Pocahontas' Descendants

A Revision, Enlargement and Extension
of the List as Set Out by
Wyndham Robertson in His Book
Pocahontas and Her Descendants (1887)

By *Stuart E. Brown, Jr.,*
Lorraine F. Myers

FOURTH AND FIFTH

Corrections
and
Additions

CLEARFIELD

Fourth Corrections and Additions to Pocahontas"Descendants
Originally published
Baltimore, Maryland, 2001

Fifth Corrections and Additions to Pocahontas' Descendants
Copyright © 2004 by The Pocahontas Foundation
All Rights Reserved.

Printed, two volumes in one, for
Clearfield Company, Inc. by
Genealogical Publishing Co., Inc.
Baltimore, Maryland
2004

International Standard Book Number: 0-8063-5242-6

Made in the United States of America

Pocahontas' Descendants

A Revision, Enlargement and Extension
of the List as Set Out by
Wyndham Robertson in His Book
Pocahontas and Her Descendants (1887)

By Stuart E. Brown, Jr.,
Lorraine F. Myers

FOURTH

Corrections
and
Additions

Acknowledgements

Much of the data included in this volume was obtained from or through the assistance of the following persons and organizations: Ethel Marlette Anepohl; Sally Moore Benson Brace; Susan Lancaster Burgess; Frances Archer Strand Caldwell; Carolyn Evans; David Harris MBE (The Greenwich Foundation for The Royal Naval College); Michael David Harrison; Andrew M. Hassell; Daniel E. Hawks (Jamestown-Yorktown Foundation); Anne Vaiden Hodges; Frederic C. Hoff; Peyton H. Hoge III; George Harrison Houston; Mary Ellen Howe; Betty A. Kean; Sidney E. King; Beth DeHardit Richardson; Charles Baskerville Saunders, Jr.; Katherine Rosborough Spicer; Margie Tucker Stewart; Michael L. Teague; Emily Evarts Vaughan; Elizabeth Lewis Carter Harrison White and Joanne Yeck.

Happening at "Bizarre"

A scandal concerning Richard Randolph (231) and his wife's sister, Ann Cary Randolph (2418), is discussed in some detail in THE RANDOLPHS. THE STORY OF A VIRGINIA FAMILY (1946) by H. J. Eckenrode and in THE BIZARRE SISTERS (1950), a novel by Jay and Audrey Walz.

Introduction

The Pocahontas Foundation, based upon information furnished to it, has compiled a tentative list of the descendants of Pocahontas, a list set forth in a combined volume (printed in 1994 and reissued in 1997) which includes reprints of the three books POCAHONTAS' DESCENDANTS (1985), CORRECTIONS AND ADDITIONS TO POCAHONTAS' DESCENDANTS (1992) and SECOND CORRECTIONS AND ADDITIONS TO POCAHONTAS' DESCENDANTS (1994). There is a separate 1997 book, THIRD CORRECTIONS AND ADDITIONS TO POCAHONTAS' DESCENDANTS and the list continues with this FOURTH CORRECTIONS AND ADDITIONS TO POCAHONTAS' DESCENDANTS.

Proposed corrections and/or additions to the list are cordially invited, and should be sent by mail (together with a stamped and addressed envelope) to The Pocahontas Foundation, P. O. Box 431, Berryville, VA 22611.

Additional Bibliography

Bolling, Mary Jane. THE BOLLING FAMILY. 1993.
POCAHONTAS QUARTERLY. Vol. 5, No. 2 (Summer 1999) and Vol. 6, No. 1 (Spring 2000).
Saunders, Charles Baskerville, Jr. FOUR CENTURIES IN AMERICA: THE BRITISH HERITAGE OF THE SAUNDERS/CARMICHAEL AND SHAFER/MCINTIRE FAMILIES. 2000.
Warden, Page Laubach. THE KIN PATCH. A PATH TO THE PAST.

Falmouth-Indian Queens

See SECOND CORRECTIONS AND ADDITIONS page iv and THIRD CORRECTIONS AND ADDITIONS page iv.

Pocahontas, her infant son and companions, leaving Falmouth by stage coach, were soon on the ancient Stanna Way or Harron Way, the Old Tin Road (which is now Route A30). At a high tollgate, Carwogie Cross, they stopped at the old Pilgrim's Inn.

This inn, where a traveller could obtain ale, cider and food and food and fodder for the horses, later became known as The Indian Queen, and the surrounding village is now called Indian Queens.

Two Pocahontas Errors

Many descendants of Pocahontas are concerned about two Pocahontas errors, the first being about her hair and her clothing or lack of clothing and the second being about her conversion to Christianity.

In the Spring of 1607, when the English colonists first settled on the island to be called Jamestown and saw Pocahontas, she probably looked somewhat like the illustration of a water color done in 1584-5 on the Carolina banks by John White of the ill-fated Roanoke Colony and appearing on the front cover of the booklet POCAHONTAS by Stuart E. Brown, Jr.

The booklet, printed in 1989 and reprinted in 1995, is referred to hereinafter as POCAHONTAS.

As noted in POCAHONTAS, the probabilities are that on the head of Pocahontas the fore part of her "grosse" and "thick" black hair was "shaven close" and the very long "thicker part" was "tied in a pleate hanging down" to her hips.

The probabilities are that Pocahontas was uncovered down to her waist, that she wore "a kind of semicinctum leathren apron (as doe our artificers or handicrafts men)", and that she was bare-footed.

In Captain John Smith's 1624 book, the "Pocahontas Saves Smith" illustration, which Smith probably approved, shows Pocahontas' back but she seems to be uncovered down to her apron and is bare-footed. See POCAHONTAS page 7.

An early, perhaps the earliest depiction of Pocahontas are two pictures done by George Keller for EIN WARHAFETIGER UND GRUNDTLICHER BERIGHT VON DEM JTZIGEN ZUSTANDT DER LANDT-SCHAFFT VIRGINIEN, a 1617 Dutch translation of Ralph Hamor's 1615 work, A TRUE DISCOURSE OF THE PRESENT STATE OF VIRGINIA.

The first of these two pictures, called "The Abduction of Pocahontas", is shown in POCAHONTAS on page 15, and depicts her partly covered down to her apron and bare-footed. This picture appears below on page 12. Courtesy Virginia State Library.

The second of these two pictures, called "Matchkot", and shown in POCAHONTAS on page 18, is reproduced below. It depicts two of the brothers of Pocahontas and she is uncovered down to her apron and bare-footed. The small colonist, probably acting as interpreter, may be Thomas Savage. Courtesy Virginia State Library.

PARS DECIMA AMERICÆ.
VIII.

Dum Indiani ab Anglis inducias impetrant, duo Regis
Powhatanis filii fororem fuam invifunt. cap.3.

Ofteaquam Angli ad præcipuam Regis Powhatanis fedem, vicum quendam Matzkot dictum perveniffent; qua-
dringenti barbari probè armati aditu illos vultu verbifque minacibus prohibere fategerunt: Nihilominus Angli,
licet iniquiore effent loco, in terram enituntur. Barbari rerum fuarum fecuri ne latum quidem unguem ipfis cedunt,
fed furfum deorfum, hac illácque inter Anglos obambulantes, præcipuos ex illis de Anglorum rege, quo animo in
las regiones deveniffent, num ferro decernendum putarent, percontabantur, interim inducias expofcentes donec ad regem
es deferretur. Quæ quidem certis conditionibus ipfis conceffæ funt. Siquidem enim minùs ex ipforum voto Rex refponfurus
fet, tubâ clafficum datum iri, ut fignis collatis hoftiliter inter fe congrederentur. Interea Pokahuntas in terram delata, à duo-
bus fratribus invifebatur, qui optimè illam inter Anglos haberi confpicati, omnem operam apud patrem fe daturos
polliciti funt, ut demum certa firmáque pax utrinque fanciretur. Atque ita Angli ab
armis difcefferunt.

A later depiction shows Pocahontas crowned but uncovered above her waist in the painting appearing on the ceiling of the upper hall in The Greenwich Foundation for the Royal Naval College at The Old Royal Navy College in Greenwich. King William and Queen Mary occupy the center and on the left Pocahontas represents the thirteen colonies.

Pocahontas, uncovered above her waist, is also shown in various illustrations appearing in such items as POCAHONTAS: HER LIFE AND LEGEND by William M. S. Rasmussen and Robert S. Tilton (1994) and THE CHILDREN'S POCAHONTAS: FROM GENTLE CHILD OF THE WORLD TO ALL-AMERICAN HEROINE by Laura Wasowicz (1996) (a reprint from The Proceedings of the American Antiquarian Society, Vol. 105, Part 2).

As regards covering, as is noted in POCAHONTAS on page 4, "The better sort of women cover them(selves) (for the most parte) all over with skyn mantells, fynely drest, shagged and frindged at the skirt, carved and coulored with some pretty work . . . of beasts, fowle, tortoyses, or other such Imagery . . . some use mantells, made both of turkey feathers and other fowle so prettely wrought and woven with threeds that nothing could be discerned but the feathers, which were exceeding warm and very handsome . . . " .

This painting of Pocahontas is estimated to date from the mid-17th Century.

As is also noted in POCAHONTAS on page 4, "sometymes in cold weather, or when they goe a hunting, or seeking the fruicts of the woodes, or gathering bents for their matts, both men and women (to defind them from the bushes) put on a kynd of leather breeches and stockings."

Perhaps the best depiction of Pocahontas being shown bare-footed and uncovered above her waist is the black and white copy of a 1960 Sidney E. King study reproduced on page iii of THIRD CORRECTIONS AND ADDITIONS.

Like several Pocahontas likenesses done by King, all echoing the 1584-5 water colors done by John White, this study was made in the preparation of a tobacco diorama for the New World Pavilion of the Jamestown Festival Park. But in the completed diorama, Pocahontas, seated on a stump beside a tobacco crop attended to by John Rolfe, does not appear as she is shown in the study. There were objections and Pocahontas is covered.

When the Jamestown Festival Park's exhibits were dismantled some years ago to make way for the Jamestown-Yorktown Foundation's new artifact-oriented museum galleries, the tobacco diorama was given to The John Rolfe Museum and Historical Research Center at John Rolfe Middle School in Henrico County, Virginia.

As regards statues, many fail to show Pocahontas as she probably existed.

Possibly the best known statue is the one at Jamestown depicted on page iv of POCAHONTAS' DESCENDANTS and duplicated in the graveyard at St. George Church in Gravesend, England. Pocahontas is shown as the many people of the early 20th Century felt that she should have looked.

A later, smaller size 1994 statue by Adolf Sehring stands in Gloucester, Virginia, at Main Street and Bellamy Road, and shows Pocahontas covered above her waist, with moccasins and with arm and ankle bands in place of tattoos.

Word has it that many of the proponents of this statue wanted Pocahontas to be moccasin-less and uncovered above her waist but strong objections prevailed.

Colored post cards of this Sehring statue are available from Princess Pocahontas Foundation, P. O. Box 675, Gloucester, VA 23061.

Perhaps the widest-seen, modern depiction of Pocahontas is "Pocahontas", the 1994 Walt Disney Studios movie which terminates in September of 1609 when Captain John Smith, accidentally and severely wounded, leaves Jamestown and returns to England.

The movie errs in countless respects including showing Pocahontas covered above her waist and wearing moccasins.

After Pocahontas' April 1613 abduction by the Colony, she probably wore such clothes as the Colonists told her to wear and the 1616 "Top Hat Engraving" done in London by Simon van de Passe shows Pocahontas in an outfit in which almost any lady would look pretty and in which almost any lady would feel miserable. Pocahontas' face probably was tattooed although such is not shown in the engraving.

Conversion to Christianity

Many persons have concluded that Pocahontas was converted to Christianity but there is substantial doubt that such was ever her fate or her blessing.

A good example of this doubt is expressed in the following portion of a piece "Curious Remarks Concerning the Savages of North America" by "Dr. B. Franklin" included in the book THE CURIOSITIES AND RARITIES ON NATURE AND ART (1794):

"The politeness of these savages in conversation, is indeed, carried to excess; since it does not permit them to contradict, or deny the truth of what is asserted in their presence. By this means they indeed avoid disputes; but then it becomes difficult to know their minds, or what impression you make upon them. The missionaries who have attempted to convert them to Christianity, all complain of this as one of the great difficulties of their mission. The Indians hear with patience the truths of the gospel explained to them, and give their usual tokens of assent and approbation: you would think they were convinced.--No such matter; it is mere civility."

Pocahontas Museum in Gloucester

Werowocomoco (Wicomico), the main village of Powhatan and Pocahontas and where Pocahontas saved the life of Captain John Smith, is located in Gloucester County, Virginia, and in Gloucester, the county seat. There Beth Dehardit Richardson heads up a splendid Pocahontas Museum which includes, among countless other Pocahontas treasures, "Smith's Rock", the stone upon which, according to legend, Captain John Smith's head was placed when Pocahontas saved his life.

Pocahontas Quarterly

Pocahontas Quarterly containing many inquires about descent from Pocahontas is edited by Beth Dehardit Richardson. Address: P. O. Box 675, Gloucester, VA 23061.

FOURTH CORRECTIONS AND ADDITIONS TO POCAHONTAS' DESCENDANTS
and/or CORRECTIONS AND ADDITIONS and/or
SECOND CORRECTIONS AND ADDITIONS and/or
THIRD CORRECTIONS AND ADDITIONS

111326541 Elizabeth Graham Hassell, m. 1987, Augustus Reeves
           Griffith
111326542 Jane Mathis Hassell, m. Keith Steven Wishon·

1113265422 Stephen Donald Wishon (4/9/1988-   )
1113265423 Michael John Wishon (4/1/1993-   )

11141821 Katherine Anne Robertson White, m. Michael C.
         Pugliese, Jr. (1955-   )
111418211 Samantha Anne Pugliese (1994-   )
111418212 Dominic Kiziah Pugliese (1996-   )

1322133 Jane Jackson of Houston (b. in Tuscumbia, AL), m.
       10/29/1885, George Washington Polk of Houston (b. in
       TN), employed by Southern Pacific R.R. (He was 49
       when 13221334 was born)

13221332 George Washington Polk, Jr. (1889-   )
13221333 Jane Jackson Polk (1893-   ), m. 9/14/1918, George
       Gill Ball in San Antonio
132213331 George Gill Ball, Jr. (1919-   ) (b. in San Antonio)
132213332 Jane Polk Ball (1923-   ) (b. in Philippines)
132213333 Harry Polk Ball (8/13/1925-   ) (b. in Cheyenne)
13221334 Harry Jackson Polk (5/16/1896-1/20/1983) (b. in
       Houston, d. Pt. Clair, AL), m. 3/1/1928, in San
       Antonio, Mildred Zachry Whitley of Texarkana, TX.
       Polk was a lawyer. (Age at time of marriage 28.)
132213341 Mildred Whitley Polk (12/17/1928-10/7/1998) (b. in
       San Antonio, d. in Kerrville, TX), m. 8/7/1948,
       in New Orleans, George Clifton Benson
1322133411 Sallie Moore Benson (2/28/1953-   ) (b. in Houston),
       m. 8/30/1974, in Houston, Thomas Alan Brace
13221334111 Jeffrey Alan Brace (10/7/1978-   ) (b. in
       Amarillo)
13221334112 Jessica Polk Brace (8/4/1980-   ) (b. in Amarillo)
1322133412 George Clifton Benson, Jr. (6/3/1954-   ) (b. in
       Houston), m. 6/11/1983, Margaret Irene Sosnowy
1322133413 Harrison Polk Benson (7/20/1957-   ) (b. in Denver)
1322133414 James Zachry Benson (2/29/1960-   ) (b. in Denver),
       m. 9/29/1984, in Houston, Vicki Love Boutwell
13221334141 Zachry Polk Benson (7/9/1989-   ) (b. in Bay City,
       TX)
13221334142 Zane Alexander Benson (9/1/1992-   ) (b. in Bay
       City, TX)
132213342 Ann Polk (11/15/1932-1980) (b. in San Antonio, d. in
       Atlanta), m. 4/12/1952, in New Orleans, John Ernest
       Sampson

1322133421 Kate Breckenridge Sampson (12/31/1957-d. of cancer),
            m. 8/5/1978, James Wendell Long
1322133422 Mimi Polk Sampson (12/16/1959-   ) (b. in Charlotte),
            m. 4/15/1978, Robert Alan McIntyre
1322133423 Anita Faye Sampson (7/19/1962-   ) (b. in Birming-
            ham)
1322133424 John Ernest Sampson, Jr. (4/17/1965-   ) (b. in
            Biloxi)

132626   Pocahontas Rebecca Cabbell Abell of Brunswick, MO (1846-
         1925), m. (1st) 1861, Dr. James E. White. No children
         surviving infancy. M. (2nd) 1878, Rev. Joseph King of
         London, England (1835-1913), son of William and Prudence
         King. Joseph King married first Nannie J. Boles (1841-
         1877) (seven children born to Joseph and Nannie King).
   Children of Pocahontas Rebecca Abell and Joseph King:
1326262 Ellen Abell King (1880-1961), m. 1912, Eugene Williams
13262621 Joseph Edward Williams (1914- ?), m. 1943, Shirley
         Skeel
132626211 dau. (b. 1947)
1326263 Mary Mariah King (1883- ?), m. 1907, Harry Holloway
13262631 Harry Holloway, Jr., m. _____
132626311
132626312
13262632 Joseph Holloway, m. _____
132626321
13262633 Mary Lou Holloway, m. James Durham
132626331
1326264 Addison Thompson King (1882-1918), m. 1906, Ruth
         Mumpower
13262641 Addison Thompson King, Jr., m. _____
132626411
132626412
132626413
132626414
132626415
13262642 Joseph King
13262643 John King (d. in infancy)
13262644 Mary Catherine King, m. Robert _____
132626441
13262645 Ruth Cabell King, m. Carl Monk
132626451
132626452
1326265 Ruth Scarritt King (11/15/1886-4/ /1971) (b. in Neosho,
         MO), m. 1911, Archie Byron Jackson (1890-1973), son of
         Virgil Davis Jackson (1829-1911) and Ida May Livermore
         (1829-1928)
13262651 Davis King Jackson (1912-199?), m. 1939, Myrtle Steward
         (1901-   ) (Myrtle Steward m. (1st) _____ Van Dyne)
132626511 Barbara Ruth Jackson (1940-   ), m. Pete Gattemeier
13262652 Archie Byron Jackson, Jr. (1913-2000), m. 1938, Willa
         Helene Kemper (1916-1976), dau. of Roy C. and Myrtle
         Morgan Kemper

132626521 Heather Diane Jackson (1939-1939)
132626522 Helene Kay Jackson also known as Kamama Tsigili (1945-
              ), m. 1963, John Edward Yeager
1326265221 Elizabeth Kay Yeager (1963-   ), m. Daryl Kuda
13262652211 Darylyn Pristine Kuda (1985?-   )
1326265222 Laurel Helene Yeager (1967-1994), m. Virgil Kempker
13262652221 John Francis Byron Kempker (1987-   )
1326265223 John Edward Yeager, Jr. (1969-   )
1326265224 Charles Jackson Yeager (1970-   )
1326265225 Morgan Hull Yeager (1973-   ), m. 1996, Stephanie
              Bosworth
13262652251 Nikita Marie Yeager (1998-   )
     Note: Adopted child of 13262652:
              Archie Byron Jackson III
13262653 Stella Lucille Jackson (1918-   ), m. 1937, Horace Lee
              Schneider (1915-199?)
132626531 Ruth Ann Schneider, m. James Case
1326265311
1326265312
        Several grandchildren
132626532 Linda Lee Schneider, m. James Grazier
1326265321
1326265322
        Several grandchildren
132626533 Dorothy Louise Schneider, m. _____
1326265331 (?)
1326265332 (?)
132626534 Horace Lee Schneider, Jr., m. _____
1326265341
1326265342

1344 Robert Markham Bolling (1795-1876), m. (4th) Frances P.
        (last name unknown) (ca. 1810-   ). His biography in
        the COLLEGE OF HAMPDEN SIDNEY DICTIONARY OF BIOGRAPHY
        states he "Lived a quiet farmer's life, a zealous
        Methodist and a good man".
     Child by first wife:
13441 Pocahontas Bolling (1825-1858) (Tombstone at Chellowe,
        Buckingham County).

     Child by fourth wife:
13442 Susan Peyton Bolling (1851-1911), m. (1st) 12/11/1879,
        Henry LeGare Cobbs (7/13/1853-4/ /1884), son of John W.
        and Sarah A. Cobbs of Buckingham County; m. (2nd) 10/28/
        1890, Richard B. Dowdy (7/ /1842-1909), son of John A.
        and Mary A. Dowdy.
     Children by first husband:
134421 John Robert Cobbs (2/1/1884-10/19/1934), m. Myrtle Maude
        Catlett (6/14/1887-3/13/1984), dau. of George R. Catlett
        (-1929) and Isabell F. Shores Catlett (1859-1942)
        of Buckingham County. John Robert changed the family
        name from Cobbs to Cobb.
1344211 George LeGarrel ("Gary") Cobb (12/30/1906-1/27/1967), m.
        Ida Davis (2/12/1916-   )

13442111   George LeGarrel Cobb, Jr., m. 4/14/1962, Rebecca
       ("Becky") Hammack, dau. of Edward Rodham and Helen
       Clark Hammack.
134421111   David Glenn Cobb (1/21/1963-   )
134421112   Tracy Renee Cobb (4/8/1966-   ), m. 9/23/1993, Andy
       Smith
13442112   Frances Maxine Cobb, m. 1961, Kenneth Marvin Leedy
134421121   Patricia Ann Leedy (12/24/1962-   )
134421122   Kenneth Michael Leedy (8/23/1965-   )
13442113   John Robert Cobb (6/14/1942-   ), m. 6/ /1964, Eloise
       Hockaday
134421131   Gary Hockaday (12/9/1966-   )
134421132   Robert Thomas Hockaday (7/ /1970-   )
13442114   Barbara Ann Cobb (10/18/1943-   ), m. 12/ /1979,
       Daniel McMahon
1344212   Frances Cobb, m. Leslie Mann
13442121   Lois Mann, m. (1st) _____ Brown; m. (2nd) Robert
       Maxwell
    Children by second husband:
134421211   Blane Maxwell
134421212   Ryan Maxwell
1344213   Blanche Cobb, m. Albert L. Thompson
1344214   Ruth Cobb, m. Harvey Cook
13442141   Gordon Terry Cook
13442142   Jesse Norman Cook
13442143   Bobby Houston Cook
1344215   Wylie Hubbard Cobb (1919-1972), m. (1st) Jean C. _____
       (3/24/1923-12/3/1964); m. (2nd) _____
    Child by first wife:
13442151   Wylie Hubbard Cobb, Jr.
    Child by second wife:
13442152   Lisa Cobb
1344216   John Oliver Cobb (twin of Olive Cobb), m. Frances Downey
1344217   Olive Cobb (twin of John Oliver Cobb), m. Clarence Davis
1344218   Bolling Alfred Cobb (8/2/1922-12/9/1991), m. Edith Burks
       (8/31/1928-   )
13442181   Brenda Gayle Cobb (5/10/1953-   ), m. (1st) Ray
       Reynolds (4/29/1952-1/4/1992); m. (2nd) Randy Mitchell
       (10/30/1945-7/ /1992); m. (3rd) Fredic C. Hof (7/14/
       1947-   )
    Child by first husband:
134421811   Ellen Brooke Reynolds (6/9/1975-   )
13442182   Michael Robert Cobb (8/25/1954-   ), m. Vicky Cyrus
134421821   Jason Michael Cobb (8/23/1985-   )
13442183   Rickey Lynn Cobb (7/18/1963-   )
134422   Infant (twin of John Robert Cobb 134421)
13443   Robert Bolling, Jr. (1846-   )
    Additional child of Robert Bolling (1344) by first wife:
13444   Lenaeus Bolling, M.D. (1822-11/ /1892 or 12/28/1893 or
       5/20/1894), M.D. of Slate River, Buckingham County, m.
       Amanda E. Harris (7/14/1829-6/7/1896), dau. of John and
       Eveline Moseley Harris of Buckingham County
134441   Sarah Pocahontas Bolling (7/25/1854-   ), m. 1874,
       Addison B. Ford

134442   Robert Langhorn Bolling (8/18/1855-7/8/1884)
134443   Mary Eleanor Bolling (12/10/1856-died young)
134444   Philip Augustus Bolling (2/11/1858-   )
134445   Amanda Elizabeth Bolling (2/27/1859-died young)
134446   Lenaeus Bolling (4/5/1860-1870)
134447   Florence Eveline Bolling (11/8/1861-2/28/1907), m.
         9/19/1888, James Wyatt McCulloch (-3/7/1893)
1344471 Lenaeus Bolling McCulloch (-4/18/1892)
1344472 R. H. McCulloch (-5/9/1936), m. Dovie Taylor
13444721 Raymond Bolling McCulloch, m. Mary _____
13444722 Florence ("Bessie") McCulloch, m. Hatch Baxendale.
         Residence: Nashville, TN
1344473 Child
134448   Louisanna Steptoe Bolling (8/8/1863-   )
134449   Virginia Argyle Harrison ("Pinkie") Bolling (2/24/1864-
         1924), m. James Skidmore of Washington, DC
1344491 James Hubbard Skidmore (1898-1971), m. Katherine Lee
         Childress (12/ /1883-1933), dau. of Joshua and Ella
         Childress of Appomattox, VA

13444911 James Lee Skidmore (1922-   ), m. 1951, Marjorie
         Louise Vaughan (1929-   )
134449111 Colin Randolph Skidmore (1963-   )
1344492 Ivanhoe Bolling Skidmore (1898-1986) of Scottsville, VA
1344493 Amanda Harris Skidmore (8/5/1896-1/14/1968), m. 1915,
         William Miller Payne (6/5/1894-1//198?) of Scottsville,
         VA
13444931 William Randolph Payne (1/14/1920-   ), m. Agnes
         Milligan (7/10/19??-   ) of Massachusetts
134449311 Mary Ellen Payne (2/22/1952-   ) m. (1st) _____;
         m. (2nd) Peter Kousis (No children by first husband)
1344493111 Kristine Kousis
1344493112 James Randolph Kousis
1344493113 Katherine Kousis
1344493114 Nichole Allison Kousis
13444932 A girl, stillborn (11/ /1918)
13444933 Amanda Virginia Payne (11/29/1922-   ) of Scottsville,
         VA, m. 10/11/1952, Conrad Livingston Hall (7/13/1925-
         9/15/1978) of NC
134449331 Amanda Katherine Hall (10/28/53-   ) of Scottsville,
         VA, m. (1st) Nicholas _____; m. (2nd) Doug Yensen
   Children by second husband:
1344493311 Laura Anne Yensen
1344493312 Johnathan Conrad Yensen
1344493313 Jennifer Hollins Yensen
134449332 Steven Jackson Hall (2/18/1956-   ) of Scottsville,
         VA
134449333 Mildred Anne Hall (11/22/1957-   ) of Charlottesville,
         VA, m. Philip Edward Hawkins (3/ /1957)
1344493331 Margaret Amanda Hawkins (3/22/1988-   )
1344493332 Katherine Anne Hawkins (12/21/1991-   )
13444934 Mildred Bolling Payne (8/24/1925-   ) of Scottsville,
         VA. Unm.

6

```
13444935   Chester Banks Payne (1/18/1928-      ) of Atlanta, GA,
           m. Jean Cain
13444936   James Bolling Payne (4/30/1930-      ) of Scottsville,
           VA. Unm.
13444x     Julian Bolling (4/10/1865-     )
13444a     Alexander Moseley Bolling (6/  /1866-      ), m. Callie
           Williams
13444a1    Alexander Bolling of Arvonia, VA, m. Virginia _____
13444a2    Rena Bolling of Scottsville, VA, m. W. M. Cook
13444b     Ivanhoe Alfonso Bolling (8/10/1870-7/13/1943), m. 2/9/
           1910, Mary Pearl Payne (10/27/1879-4/14/1948).  Both of
           Buckingham County, VA
13444b1    Mary Amanda Bolling (7/4/1911-4/25/1984) of Florida and
           Manassas, VA, m. Raymond Simard
13444b11   Lorraine Simard (12/19/1944-      ) of Florida, m. Simon
           Casoria
13444b111  Darrell Casoria (1965-     )
13444b112  Simon Casoria (Jr.)

13444b2    Nathan Leneas Bolling (3/6/1913-3/2/1989) of Manassas,
           VA, m. 3/  /1947, Irma Richardson (8/9/1911-      ) of
           Buckingham County
13444b21   Philip Ivanhoe Bolling (10/22/1951-      ) of Manassas,
           VA, m. 9/3/1983, Bonni Van Fleet (4/1/1959-     )
13444b211  Holly Sue Bolling (1/30/1985-      ) of Manassas, VA
13444b3    Robert Glover Bolling (7/8/1915-10/8/1984) of Richmond,
           VA, m. 7/7/1950, Elizabeth Snoddy (9/20/1916-7/7/1966)
           of Arvonia, VA
13444b31   Joan Elizabeth Bolling (7/24/1953-      ) of Richmond,
           VA, m. 10/21/1972, James Durwood Stargardt (11/14/
           1945-     ) of Richmond, VA
13444b311  Stacie Elizabeth Stargardt (7/15/1974-      )
13444b312  Leslie Bolling Stargardt (11/30/1977-     )
13444b32   Mary Jane Bolling (3/7/1960-     ) of Richmond, VA,
           m. 3/21/1981,  Carlton Ray Anderson (5/9/1957-     )
           of Chatham, VA.  Div. 10/  /1986.  No children.
13444b33   Robert Glover Bolling, Jr. (10/26/1955-      ) of Burke-
           ville, VA, m. 9/21/1974, Jessie Lee Keys (10/22/1955-
           ) of Arvonia, VA
13444b331  Robert Shawn Bolling (2/22/1979-     )
13444b332  Brandon Lee Bolling (11/1/1981-     )
13444b333  Douglas William Bolling (6/9/1987-     )
13444b4    Nell Bolling (12/23/1917-     ) of Richmond, VA, m. (1st)
           Bill Findley; m. (2nd) Francis E. Zacharias (1916-1975)
     Child by first husband:
13444b41   Cleo Patricia Findley (10/13/1942-     ) of Tallahassee,
           FL, m. Steve Freeman.  Divorced - no children)
     Child by second husband:
13444b42   Franel Edre Zacharias (7/8/1958-      ) of Richmond, VA

NOTE:  13444 and his wife, Amanda E. Harris Bolling are buried in
       the Bolling cemetery in Buckingham County, on Route  652,
       as are 134442, 134449, 13444x, 13444a and his wife, Pearl
       Payne Bolling.
```

1345 Lenaeus Bolling, Jr. (ca. 1800-1816). Drowned 1816 in a
      boating accident while at William & Mary College, where he
      was a student.

NOTE: Eliminate 13451, 13452 and 13453

135 Powhatan Bolling (1767-3/21/1803). A locket containing a
     miniature portrait is owned by Mrs. Brenda Hof (13442181).
     Inscribed on the back of the locket, spelling errors and
     all, are the words "Ex Persona Bollingg a Auropaque a. suae
     24 1791." He was, therefore, 24-years-old when the locket
     was made in 1791. Auropaque is a Latinized rendering of
     Oropaks, an encampment along the Chickahominy River of
     Pocahontas' father. Powhatan Bolling stood for Congress
     in the Prince Edward district in 1799 and was defeated by
     John Randolph. His obituary is in the 4/9/1803 edition of
     the VIRGINIA ARGUS.

1751121 Byrd Willis Hopkins, m. (1st) Katherine Rosborough.
        Div. She is now Mrs. Spicer.

17511213 William Rosborough Hopkins

PRESENTATION OF POCAHONTAS AT COURT.

212214   Lingan Strother Randolph (b. Martinsburg, d. Baltimore)

2122142   Orlando Robbins Randolph (b. Blacksburg, VA - d.
          Charlottesville, 4/15/1970), m. at Warm Springs, VA,
          Jean Graham McAllister (b. Warm Springs, VA - d.
          Charlottesville, 3/1/1988)
21221421 Beverley Randolph (b. Brooklyn, d. Charlottesville,
          5/29/1994), m. Charlottesville, 12/15/1951, William
          Wilder Westbury Knight (b. Punta Gorda, FL, 1/18/1922-
          d. St. Petersburg, 9/1/1982)
212214211 Mary Sommers Knight (2/22/1953-   ), m. Toluca,
          Mexico, 4/16/1980, Jose Guillero Estrada
2122142111 Noel Josefino Estrada (b. Toluca, Mexico, 10/5/1982-
)
2122142112 William Gustavo Estrada (b. Riverside, CA, 5/17/1985-
)
212214212 William Wilder Knight, Jr. (6/13/1955-   ), m. Bad
          Durkheim, Germany, Gabrille Dehn (3/1/1956-   )
2122142121 Maxmilian Gabriel Dehn Knight (b. Brooklyn, 9/1/1993-
)
2122142122 Emily Rachel Dehn Knight (b. New York, NY, 11/13/
          1990-   )
212214213 Randolph Robbins Knight (4/18/1961-   ), m. 7/5/1986,
          Grace Spenser Wells (12/16/1960-   )
2122142131 Samuel Sturdivant Knight (b. Bryn Mawr, 1/3/1988-
)
2122142132 Abel McAllister Knight (b. Charlottesville, 4/13/
          1990-   )
21221422 Jean Graham Randolph (b. Brooklyn, 10/7/1929-   ),
          m. Charlottesville, 6/21/1952, Alan Martin Bruns
          (4/16/1927-   ). Div. October 1972.
212214221 Bryan Randolph Bruns (b. Charlottesville, 2/1/1956-
          ), m. Bangkok, Thailand, 12/29/1981, Papking
          Chalad Daun Ngeun (Silver Hill) (b. Phyao Province,
          Thailand, 1/12/1959-   )
2122142211 Lily Busaba Bruns (b. Jakarta, Indonesia, 10/25/
          1989-   )
2122142212 Robin Chalad Bruns (b. Chiang Mai, Thailand, 6/21/
          1993-   )
    Note: Bryan Randolph Bruns has a stepson, Natapong
          Sappermpurn (b. Bangkok, Thailand, 3/20/1980-   )
212214222 Mary Anderson Bruns (b. Charlottesville, 12/11/1958-
          ), m. (1st) 1981, Michael O'Dell, m. (2nd)
          Silver Springs, Md., 12/19/1992, Lindsay Asay (4/24/
          1957-   )
2122142221 Alma O'Dell (6/14/1982-   ). Last name changed
          to Asay following her mother's second marriage.
2122142222 Logan O'Dell (4/23/1984-   ). Last name changed
          to Asay following her mother's second marriage.

2223 Patrick Henry Randolph
22231 Mary Susan Randolph, b. "Chaumiere", m. Robert Barnhart
      (1822-   ) from Barnhart's Island, Canada

222312   William Randolph Barnhart (1850-   ), m. 1884, Fannie
        Greenwood Woodson
2223121   Robert Everard Barnhart (1895-1975), m. 1937, America
        Hathaway Price (1915-1981)
22231211 Margaret Woodson Barnhart (2/21/1939-   ), m. 6/20/
        1963, James Steirling Gunn (1/11/1934-   )
222312111 Nancy Randolph Gunn (6/16/1966-   ) (b. Williamsburg,
        VA), m. 7/5/1995 (at Manakin Church, Powhatan, VA),
        Curtis Stephen Colden
222312112 Elizabeth Purnell Gunn (9/25/1968-4/7/1991). B. in
        Richmond, d. in Boston. Bur. Manakin Church,
        Powhatan, VA.
2223122
2223123
2223124
2223125
2223126
2223127

24142x113   Jane Kean Randolph Butler (b. and d. in New Orleans),
        m. Wesley Cleo Lancaster (9/5/1902-11/29/1963) (b. in
        Paragould, AR, d. in Alexandria, LA), son of Henry
        Monroe and Suzane Harriet Whipple Lancaster.
24142x1131 Wesley Cary Lancaster (b. and d. in Baton Rouge)
24142x1132 Susan Jane Lancaster (6/15/1944-   ) (b. in
        Vicksburg), m. 12/16/1962, in New Orleans, Thomas
        Burgess (9/8/1944-   ) (b. in Waynesboro, MS)
24142x11321 Evelyn Joyce Burgess (11/8/1962-   ) (b. in New
        Orleans), m. 1/15/1993, in Metairie, LA, Ernest
        Rogers (2/8/1944-   )
24142x113211 Sharon Nicole Rogers (1/26/1988-   ) (b. in
        Metairie, LA)
24142x11322 Marilyn Rene Burgess (3/23/1964-   ) (b. in New
        Orleans), m. 7/15/1984 in Kenner, LA, Anthony
        O'Dell James (1/1/1947-   ) (b. in Laurel, MS).
        Div. April, 1999
24142x113221 Amanda Rene James (12/20/1982-   ) (b. in New
        Orleans)
24142x113222 Suzzane Joyce James (2/18/1984-   ) (b. in New
        Orleans)
24142x113223 Anthony O'Dell James, Jr. (1/27/1986-   ) (b. in
        New Orleans)
24142x11323 Kathleen Rochelle Burgess (5/12/1965-   ) (b. in
        New Orleans), m. 8/10/1985 in Metairie, LA, Leon
        John Russo III (12/12/1964-   )
24142x113231 Vickie Lynn Russo (3/3/1986-   ) (b. in Metairie,
        LA
24142x113232 Child (b. and d. 12/25/1995 in Metairie, LA)
24142x113233 Leon John Russo IV (6/3/1997-   ) (b. in Metairie,
        LA
24142x11324 Susan Jane Burgess (7/24/1966-   ) (b. in New
        Orleans), met 1983 in Kenner, LA, Calvin Paul
        Verdun (8/12/1967-   ) (b. in New Orleans), son
        of Victor Raymond and Yvonne Mary Ortis Verdun

24142x113241   Thomas Walter Burgess (9/16/1984-   ) (b. in New Orleans)

24142x113242   Angel Marie Burgess (5/26/1986-   ) (b. in Metairie, LA)

24142x113243   Susan Jane Burgess (1/15/1988-   ) (b. in New Orleans)

24142x11325   Thomas Burgess, Jr. (9/22/1967-   ) (b. in Jackson, MS), met 1990 in Kenner, LA, Janet Elsie Hurst (6/29/1974-   ) (b. in Oklahoma City), dau. of John Wesley (Jr.) and Gail Patricia Mahaney Hurst; m. (1st) 10/18/1997, in Kenner, LA, Lisette Marie Rodrigue (3/10/1974-   ) (b. in Fort Polk, LA), dau. of Archie (Jr.) and Mary Thersea Ponthious Rodigue.

Children by Janet Elsie Hurst:

24142x113251   Christina Rachelle Burgess (9/1/1991-   ) (b. in New Orleans)

24142x113252   Joshua Dean Burgess (2/9/1995-   ) (b. in Metairie, LA)

Child by Lisette Marie Rodrigue:

24142x113253   Thomas Burgess III (9/3/1998-   ), (b. in Metairie, LA)

24142x11326   Larisa Jane Burgess (2/18/1973-   ) (b. in Jackson, MS), m. 4/18/1997, in Metairie, LA, John Patrick Gaffney, Jr. (1/1/1972-   ) (b. in Great Lakes, IL), son of John Patrick and Doretta Betz Gaffney

24142x113261   Bali Nicole Burgess (12/21/1995-   ) (b. in Metairie, LA)

24142x113262   John Austin Burgess (3/1/1997-   ) (b. in Metairie, LA

24142x11327   Lisa Grace Burgess (2/18/1973-   ) (b. in Jackson, MS)

24142x113271   Chaylor Blaine Burgess (11/16/1998-3/27/1999) (b. and d. in Kenner, LA)

24142x1133   William Joseph Lancaster (10/29/1945-1/8/1999) (b. in Vicksburg and d. in St. Rose, LA), m. (1st) 3/19/1976, in Medidian, MS, Ada Carol Littlefield (9/23/1949-   ) (b. in Tahlequah, OK), dau. of J. C. and Patsy Lee Townsend Littlefield; m. (2nd) 5/18/1991, in St. Rose, LA, Gail Patricia Mahaney, dau. of   and Peggy Rachel Mahaney.

The following children of Ada Carol Littlefield by her first marriage were adopted by William Joseph Lancaster 10/12/1977 in Japan:

   Carol Annette Lancaster (10/6/1968-   ) (b. in Key West, FL

   Laura Lee Lancaster (6/10/1971-   ) (b. in Tahlequah, OK

Children by first wife:

24142x11331   Ada Chantel Lancaster (2/18/1977-   ) (b. in Yokosuka, Japan), m. 2/3/1997 in Norfolk, VA, Eric John Morley (12/25/1975-   ) (b. in Granby, MA), son of Lawrence Roger (Sr.) and Beaverly Ann Sabourin Morley

24142x113311 Suzette Littledove Morley (10/3/1995-   ) (b. in
              Norfolk, VA)
24142x11332 Joseph Antonio Lancaster (4/10/1979-   ) (b. in
              Kokosuka, Japan)

24142x15 Mary Evalina Sanfrosa Prescott Kean (d. 4/ /1988, in
          Washington, DC)

24142x173 John Michael Kean, m. 10/8/1982, Betty Faye Miller
           (5/4/1961-   ). Home: Gonzales, LA
24142x1731 Brittney Nicole Kean (4/1/1986-   )

2421541 Agnes Rogers Page (-1953). Unm.
2421542 Mary Frances Page (-1957). Unm.
2421543 Robert Powell Page IV. Removed to Philadelphia.
         President of Autocar Co.
24215431 Robert Powell Page V, m. Margaret Hunter Lewis. Div.

242154321 Helen Hamilton Page (Dr.), m. Jan Ting
2421543211 Margaret Page Le Ching Ting
2421543212 Mary Judith Le Yun Ting
242154322 Mary Frances Page
2421544 George Burwell Page. Unm.
2421545 Nathaniel Burwell Page. Removed to "Minturn". D. un-
         expectedly of pneumonia.

242154511 Col. John Henderson Farrar, Jr., m. (1st) Dorothy
           Virginia Genau. Div. M. (2nd) Tamar Agmon
2421545111 John Henderson Farrar III, m. Jessie Bel Summerville
24215451111 John Summerville Farrar
24215451112 Leah Summerville Farrar
24215451113 Emily Summerville Farrar
24215451114 Olivia Summerville Farrar
2421545112 Frederick Lyon Farrar, m. Karen Sue Rice
24215451121 Magen Rice Farrar
2421545113 Douglas Patch Farrar, m. Virginia Martinisi-Moglia.
            Div.
2421545114 Virginia Lee Farrar, m. Maj. Keith Alan Rivenbark
24215451141 Douglas Coan Rivenbark
24215451142 Elizabeth Lyon Rivenbark
2421545115 Ilan William Farrar
2421545116 Sharon Mabel Farrar
24215452 Nathaniel Burwell Page, Jr. (-1992). Removed to
          Chevy Chase, MD. Div. 1958
242154521 Mary Catherine Page. Removed to Calvert County, MD;
           to Greenville, NC; and to Kent County, MD. M. (1st)
           1963, Frederick McOwen Middleton, Jr. (1935-1977), m.
           (2nd) 1988, Benjamin Klaus Raphael
2421545211 Frederick McOwen Middleton III (1965-   ). Removed
            to Florence, SC, and Burlington, VT. M. (1st) 1992,
            Pamela Gohrband Pierson. Div. 1995. M. (2nd) 1998,
            Christa Ann Wells
24215452111 Connor Ryan Middleton (1999-   )

242154522   Frances Byrne Page, m. 1966, Morris J. Ambrose.
            Removed to Lexington, KY; to Albany, NY; and to
            Denver, CO.
2421545221 Gordon J. Ambrose
2421545222 Andrew Kane Ambrose, m. Chandra Faith Connell
24215452221 Amanda Page Ambrose
24215452222 Alexander J. Ambrose
2421545223 Adam Morris Ambrose
242154523   Henrietta King Page, m. (1st) Michael David Aguda.
            Div. M. (2nd) Victor Kestutis Bakunas
2421545231 Mary Page Bakunas

2424173921 Michael David Harrison (/ /1956-   ). Mayor,
            Town of Claremont, VA

242445   Virginia Randolph ("Mere") Harrison (3/31/1834-8/9/1895),
            m. 2/7/1855, Rev. William James Hoge (8/14/1825-7/6/
            1864). A chaplain in the Confederate States Army.
            Died in service.

2424452   Rev. Peyton Harrison Hoge (d. 10/12/1040), m. 8/22/1883,
            Mary Stuart Holladay (2/3/1862-3/9/1949). She is
            219311.
24244521   Virginia Randolph Bolling Hoge (6/8/1884-5/4/1937), m.
            8/8/1906 in San Germano, Emidio Marchese (b. Arpino,
            Italy-d. 1860).
242445211   Mary ("Mary San") Randolph Marchese (6/7/1907-8/24/
            1989), m. Warwick McNair Anderson (9/21/1902-4/2/
            1976)
2424452111 Mary Stuart ("Stuey") Anderson, m. 10/23/1948, George
            Waldo Emerson (3/10/1918-   )
24244521111 Mary Randolph Emerson (5/19/1950-   ), m. Robert
            Wiggins (3/7/1955-   )
242445211111 Mary Stuart ("Story") Wiggins (1/1/1986-   )
24244521112 George Waldo Emerson, Jr. (7/3/1953)
2424452112 Nancy Lewis Anderson (10/17/1934-   ), m. 6/25/
            1955, Adlai Ewing Stevenson, Jr. (10/7/1930-   )
24244521121 Adlai Ewing Stevenson III (11/4/1956-   )
24244521122 Lucy Wallace Stevenson (7/2/1958-   ), m. 9/23/1989,
            Chris Neher (8/30/1957-   )
242445211221 Katie Neher (3/26/1991-   )
242445211222 Anna Neher (10/19/1993-   )
24244521123 Katherine Randolph Stevenson (4/5/1960-   ), m.
            8/ /1998, Larry Kramer
242445211231 Maxwell Bearish Kramer (7/ /1999-   )
24244521124 Warwick Lewis Stevenson (1/17/1962-   ), m. Deborah
            Stevenson
24244522   William Lacy Hoge (d. 9/27/1977), m. (1st) Emily Tryon
            Mengel (3/17/1892-8/1/1953); m. (2nd) 10/19/1957,
            Elizabeth Tinsley Campbell (d. 3/ /1993)
242445221   Emily Tryon Hoge, m. (1st) 6/9/1938, Alexander Galt
            Booth (5/4/1908-11/13/1987); m. (2nd) 6/18/1988,
            George Harrison Houston, Jr. (9/29/1914-   )

2424452211 Julia Mengel Booth (4/18/1940-5/23/1997), m. (1st)
            2/29/1964, Donald Davis Cooke; m. (2nd) 10/29/1989,
            John Craik Lord (5/31/1935-   )
242445222   Mary Holladay Hoge (d. 11/18/1992), m. 6/22/1939,
            George Kearsley Selden (6/27/1917-12/29/1985)
2424452221 Andrew Kennedy Selden II (9/19/1942-   ), m. 10/31/
            1970, Pamella Bartlett Hettrick (4/15/1944-   )
24244522211 Christopher Stewart Selden (4/9/1975-   )
24244522212 Elizabeth Bartlett Selden (7/10/1978-   )
2424452222 William Randolph Selden (7/31/1946-   ), m. (1st)
            Laura Rebecca Herrick (8/2/1947-   ); m. (2nd)
            7/24/1993, Daphne Murdock
2424452223 Emily Stewart Selden (9/27/1950-   ), m. 6/12/1971,
            Clarence Warren ("Larry") Walker (9/27/1950-   )
24244522231 Clarence Warren Walker, Jr. (9/10/1972-   )
24244522232 Stewart Seldon Walker (8/21/1974-   )
24244522233 Jenny Caroline Walker (6/21/1977-   )
242445223   William Lacy Hoge, Jr., m. (1st) 6/29/1946, Dorothy
            Dean O'Brien (1/25/1925-11/27/1990); m. (2nd) 11/7/
            1991, Edith Louise ("Jonnie") Johnson Vatter (2/24/
            1926-   )
2424452231 William Lacy Hoge III (3/28/1947-   ), m. 5/19/1989,
            Carolyn Hill (1/16/1960-   )
24244522311 Alexandra Anne Hoge (8/3/1994-   )
2424452232 Anne Holladay Hoge (7/17/1948-7/27/1953)
2424452233 Mary O'Brien Hoge (5/25/1952-   ), m. 8/3/1974,
            Charles Edward Moore
24244522331 Lacy O'Brien Moore (8/8/1986-   )
2424452234 Dorothy Holladay Hoge (1/3/1956-   ), m. 7/16/1988,
            Arthur Paul Crotty (10/20/1952-   )
24244522341 Robert William Crotty (7/2/1993-   )
24244522342 Anne Holladay Crotty (7/8/1995-   )
2424452235 Jane Lacy Hoge (8/26/1960-   ), m. 3/1/1986, David
            Charles Walker (2/7/1960-   )
24244522351 Jane Holladay Walker (11/11/1988-   )
24244522352 William O'Brien Walker (7/30/1991-   )
24244522353 Charles Patterson Walker (10/26/1995-   )
24244523   Mary Stuart Hoge (d. 4/27/1977), m. George Harrison
            Houston (1/4/1883-7/9/1949)
242445231   Peyton Hoge Houston (d. 3/8/1994), m. (1st) 11/26/
            1942, Priscilla Stewart Moore (who had two Stewart
            children); m. (2nd) 5/22/1959, Parrish Cummings
            Dobson (6/14/1916-12/23/1996) (who had three Dobson
            children).
242445232   George Harrison ("Harry") Houston, Jr. m, 6/26/1943,
            Dorothy ("Dolly") Cromwell Fielden (6/7/1913-8/27/
            1987)
2424452321 Dorothy Holladay ("Holly") Houston (10/11/1944-   ),
            m. 8/23/1969, Fredrick Kurt Knauert (8/15/1943-   )
24244523211 David Cromwell Knauert (9/13/1971-   ), m. 8/13/
            1995, Leigh Anne Kettler (9/24/1970-   )
242445232111 Peter Fredrick Knauert (10/28/1998-   )
242445232112

24244523212 Melissa Pauline Knauert (4/4/1974-   )
2424452322 George Harrison ("Harrison") Houston III (10/6/1945-
            ), m. 12/23/1967, Lynn Luise Ely (8/12/1946-
)
24244523221 Noel Luise Houston (8/12/1968-   ), m. 11/21/1992,
            Ian Dwyer (7/29/1966-   )
242244523221 William Jackson ("Jack") Dwyer (6/14/1997-   )
242244523212 Sarah Luise Dwyer (1/2/1999-   ) (identical twin)
242244523213 Grace Ashley Dwyer (1/1/1999-   ) (identical twin)
24244523222 Ashley Holladay Houston (8/2/1970-   )
2424452323 Edward ("Ned") Randolph Houston (4/24/1947-   ), m.
            1/31/1970, Susan Day Farwell (12/23/1947-   )
24244523231 Seth Farwell Houston (8/15/1974-   )
24244523232 Serin Day Houston (6/2/1978-   )
242445233 Mary Stuart ("Stuey") Houston (10/28/1918-3/12/1993),
            m. 10/12/1940, John Williams Meriwether (?/10/1912-
            1/26/1996)
2424452331 John Williams Meriwether, Jr. (4/14/1942-   ), m.
            8/18/1973, Erica Tanasijczuk (3/1/1942-   )
24244523311 Alexander Williams Meriwether (7/14/1980-   )
2424452332 Mary ("Mimi") Stuart Meriwether (11/13/1944-1/18/
            1997)
2424452333 George Houston Meriwether (2/22/1951-   )
2424452334 Cary Mead Meriwether (7/2/1954-   ), m. Kathy
            Weddell (11/20/1955-   ) (Kathy had a child whose
            last name was Finnegan)
24244523341 Elizabeth Ellen Meriwether (7/15/1982-   )
24244523342 Laura Stuart Meriwether (12/12/1984-   )
24244523343 Mary Stuart Meriwether (6/26/1987-   )
24244524 Peyton Harrison Hoge, Jr. (d. 4/27/1977), m. Blanche
            Weissinger Smith (9/24/1891-4/4/1980)
242445241 Peyton Harrison Hoge III, m. 12/23/1941, Elizabeth Ann
            Harris (1/9/1918-   ). Hoge is Mayor of Anchorage,
            KY.
2424452411 Peyton ("Peyho") Harrison Hoge IV (3/27/1943-   ), m
            (1st) 8/28/1965, Judith Ellen Breen (10/6/1942-   );
            m. (2nd) 4/14/1995, Theresa ("Terri") Cookson (5/17/
            1939-   )
24244524111 Amanthis Bullitt Hoge (9/19/1970-   )
24244524112 Peyton Harrison Hoge V (3/31/1974-   )
2424452412 George Weissinger Smith Hoge (8/24/1947-   ), m.
            6/23/1973, Doris Dee Daugherty (9/22/1951-   )
24244524121 Sarah Britton Hoge (3/2/1975-   ), m. 2/5/2000,
            Jeremy Jay Buhl
24244524122 Catherine Carlisle Hoge (4/15/1981-   )
24244524123 George Stuart Hoge (3/29/1984-   )
2424452413 Elizabeth ("Libba") Knight Hoge (11/23/1959-   ), m.
            2/13/1974, Richard Bernard Hageman, Jr. (1/18/1950-
)
24244524131 Richard Bernard Hageman III (8/31/1979-   )
24244524132 James Hoge Hageman (12/31/1981-   )
2424452414 Blanche Smith Hoge (9/5/1952-   ), m. 12/27/1977,
            Joseph H. Pedigo III (5/6/1951-   )

24244524141 Blanche ("Bambi") Weissinger Smith Pedigo (5/16/
        1980-   )
24244524142 Heather Palmer Knight Pedigo (4/12/1982-   )
2424452415 Margaret Knight Hoge (7/19/1954-   ), m. 10/18/
        1975, Robert Willis Gerhart, Jr. (12/30/1952-   )
24244524151 Elizabeth Ann Gerhart (7/4/1977-   )
24244524152 Virginia Buchanan Gerhart (5/24/1980-   )
242445242 Nell Hunt Hoge, m. 1/2/1943, Thomas Kennedy Helm, Jr.
        (9/16/1918-   )
2424452421 Thomas Kennedy Helm III (7/2/1946-   ), m. 5/30/
        1970, Elizabeth Jennifer Schmick (2/8/1946-   )
24244524211 Thomas Kennedy Helm IV (12/4/1974-   )
24244524212 Mary Emily Mitchell Helm (7/7/1978-   )
2424452422 Peyton Randolph Helm (1/30/1949-   ), m. 7/12/1980,
        Patricia Burton (9/12/1948-   )
24244524221 Randolph Burton Helm (11/8/1982-   )
24244524222 Alexander Veasy Helm (6/19/1995-   )
2424452423 Hunt Choteau Helm (3/21/1953-   ), m. (1st) 7/1/
        1978, Debra Connoll (10/1/1958-   ); m. (2nd) 3/5/
        1983, Kay Stewart (7/18/1953-   )
  Children by second wife:
24244524231 Ben Helm (8/13/1984-   )
24244524232 Charles Helm (2/18/1989-   )
24244525 Elizabeth Addison Hoge (1/17/1891-11/ /1983), m.
        Edmond Taylor Meriwether (6/25/1881-12/7/1961)
242445251 Elizabeth Hoge Meriwether, m. 5/5/1938, Stanley Carter
        Schuler (2/28/1915-   )
2424452511 Elizabeth Ashley Schuler (3/27/1941-   ), m. (1st)
        2/27/1965, Thomas Peter Rooney (6/29/1932-5/29/
        1998); m. (2nd) 10/6/1999, Peter Lund
24244525111 Elizabeth Siobhan Rooney (10/13/1966-   ), m. 8/10/
        1996, Douglas Theriault
24244525112 Stephen Loring Rooney (6/11/1968-   )
2424452512 Miranda Blake Schuler (3/12/1944-   ), m. 10/14/
        1967, William Brown Burnett (10/19/1942-   )
24244525121 William Brown Burnett, Jr. (2/22/1970-   ), m.
        11/4/1995, Sigrid Anne Croft (6/14/1969-   )
24244525122 Elizabeth Blake Burnett (6/17/1972-   )
2424452513 Cary Meriwether Schuler (9/23/1946-   ), m. 9/19/
        1970, Charles Lewis Hull (12/6/1938-   )
24244525131 Katherine Schuler Hull (1/9/1973-   )
24244525132 David Sanders Hull (1/16/1975-   )
242445252 Mary ("Maizy") Randolph Meriwether (d. 12/9/1969), m.
        (1st) 5/27/1941, Robert Parker McElwain (9/5/1917-
              ); m. (2nd) 1/20/1950, Hugh McKee Rose (d. 11/
        13/1970)
2424452521 Elizabeth ("Betsy") Kent McElwain (7/30/1944-   ),
        m. 6/29/1974, Randolph Powell Johnston
24244525211 Oliver Perry Alford Johnston (10/9/1977-   )
24244525212 George Randolph Kent Johnston (3/29/1981-   )
24244525213 Laura Tucker Powell Johnston (10/17/1984-   )
24244526 Cary Evelyn Hoge (d. 7/15/1990), m. George Jackson Mead
        (12/27/1891-1/20/1949)

242445261 George Nathaniel Jackson ("Jack") Mead, m. (1st)
        10/23/1945, Katherine Billingsley Wathen; m. (2nd)
        8/13/1997, Carole K. Rossley (7/29/1938-   )
  Children by first wife:
2424452611 Charles ("Chip") Jackson Mead (9/1/1949-   ), m.
        8/4/1978, Mary Novicki (12/25/1956-   )
2424452612 Virginia ("Ginger") Randolph Mead (7/2/1953-   ),
        m. 5/18/1974, Thomas Henry Schmitt (7/15/1947-   )
24244526121 Thomas Jefferson Schmitt (1/2/1976-   )
24244526122 Kimberly Ruth Schmitt (7/4/1977-   )
24244526123 Rebecca Lena Schmitt (7/6/1979-   )
24244526124 Katherine Mary Schmitt (9/23/1981-   )
2424452613 Cary Wathen Mead (5/9/1956-   )
2424452614 Barbara Hoge Mead (4/25/1962-   )
  Child by second wife:
2424452615 Jonathan Rossley Mead (12/30/1980-   )
242445262 Mary Randolph Mead (d. 4/12/1998), m. 10/29/1960,
        David Alexander James
242445263 Peyton Hoge Mead, m. (1st) 6/25/1949, Sarah ("Sally")
        Clark Noyes (8/13/1927-   ); m. (2nd) 1/7/1991,
        Marjorie ("Mimi") Gunn Patterson
2424452631 Morgan Noyes Mead (6/15/1950-   )
2424452632 Merrill Fowler Mead (10/14/1953-   ), m. 8/7/1982,
        David Fox (10/14/1953-   )
24244526321 Alexander Mead-Fox (2/6/1986-   )
24244526322 Nicholas Peyton Mead-Fox (5/27/1991-   )
2424452633 Caroline Jackson Mead (6/13/1955-   ), m. 7/1/1978,
        Marc Gunnels
24244526331 Laura Gunnels (6/12/1982-   )
24244526332 Jennifer Gunnels (6/9/1984-   )
24244526333 Brandon Gunnels (12/18/1986-   )
2424452634 George Jackson ("Jack II") Mead (8/21/1960-   )
242445264 Charles Cary Mead (7/4/1935-   ), 6/20/1959, Carol
        Ann Vieth (10/11/1937-   )
2424452641 Jeremy ("Jerry") Stewart Mead (10/11/1961-   )
2424452642 Elizabeth ("Betsy") Ellen Mead (2/7/1964-   )
2424452643 Robert ("Bob") Andrew Mead (5/26/1965-   ), m.
        9/13/1991, Tracy Thompson (1/24/1965-   )
24244526431 Miranda Chefna Carolyn Mead (2/22/1994-   )
242445265 William Randolph Lacy Mead (7/7/1938-   ), m. 12/23/
        1958, Johanna ("Hansy") Henriette Jacoba Van Andel
        (3/24/1936-   )
2424452651 Jan ("Jay") Willem Mead (2/15/1960-   ), m. 9/8/
        1980, Edith ("Edie") Farwell (2/1/1960-   )
24244526511 Jacob Farwell ("Cedar") Mead (8/14/1995-   )
24244526512 Silas Jan Farwell Mead (1/30/1998-   )
2424452652 Mark Nathaniel Mead (9/6/1961-   ), m. 10/10/1992,
        Elizabeth ("Sabine") Harmon (1/29/1962-   )
24244526521 Tristan William Wade Mead (6/27/1995-   )
2424452653 Samuel ("Sam") Aldo Mead (11/25/1962-   ), m. 9/17/
        1994, Katherine Elizabeth Craig (2/26/1965-   )
2424452654 Sonya Henrietta Mead (3/24/1964-   ), m. 5/30/1993,
        Alexander Whiting (8/11/1964-   )
24244526541 Matia Odette Whiting (8/15/1997-   )

```
24244526542  Noah Charles Whiting (1/27/2000-    )
2424452655   Tanya Georgine Mead (9/11/1965-    )
2424452656   Roanna Margot Mead (3/12/1967-4/20/1984)
2424452657   Anoushka Odette Mead (8/13/1976-8/26/1989)
2424452658   Joshua ("Josh") Onni Franciscus Mead (7/20/1978-    )

242453b1112  Mariah Stanard Evarts (10/3/1985-    )
242453b1113  Susanna Dashiel Evarts (4/14/1988-    )
242453b112   Jane Randolph Evarts (1/7/1953-    )
242453b113   Emily McFadden Evarts (8/21/1954-    )
242453b1131  Maxwell Evarts Vaughan (8/13/1986-    )
242453b1132  Katherine Danielle Vaughan (1/1/1989-    )
242453b1133  Nicolas Stetson Vaughan (1/25/1992-    )
242453b114   Thomas W. M. Evarts (4/5/1957-    )
242453b1141  Sophie M. Evarts (2/24/1990-    )
242453b1142  Alexandra M. Evarts (6/19/1991-    )
242453b1143  Remi J. Evarts (4/27/1994-    )
242453b115   John Randolph Harrison Evarts (2/13/1959-    ), m.
               Kathleen Kearns
242453b1151  Harrison William Evarts (3/15/1991-    )
242453b1152  Darragh Patricia Evarts (3/14/1993-    )

25163113   Frances Archer McCandlish (10/24/1924-    ), m. Frank
             Louis Strand (4/22/1925-    ), son of Peter Strand
             from Skien,  Norway and Dagmar Christine Rasmussen
             Strand from Chicago, IL.
251631131  Frances Archer Strand (7/15/1950-    ), m. 3/21/1970,
             Mason Blake Caldwell III (2/9/1946-    ), son of
             Mason Blake (Jr.) and Jean Elizabeth Moore Caldwell
             of Portsmouth, VA
2516311311  Mason Blake Caldwell IV (5/20/1981-    )
2516311312  Louisa Archer Caldwell (2/16/1985-9/12/1985)
2516311313  Jessie Samantha Caldwell (2/17/1989-    )
251631132  Robert William Strand (12/7/1951-    ), m. 8/30/1972,
             Elizabeth Ann Albrecht (12/12/1952-    ), dau. of
             Harold Lloyd Albrecht and his wife of Richmond.
2516311321  Peter Albrecht Strand (10/23/1982-    )
2516311322  Andrew Michael Strand (2/23/1985-    )
251631133  Elizabeth Whipple Strand (1/20/1953-3/30/1998)
251631134  Susan Holt Strand (11/12/1954-    ), m. 8/28/1982,
             David Randolph Wilson of Pottersville, NJ
2516311341  Ross Patrick Wilson (3/18/1984-    )
2516311342  Kelly Robyn Wilson (1/26/1987-    )
251631135  Katherine Dagmar Strand (5/28/1960-    )
```

                    3 Mary Bolling, m. Col. John Fleming

In POCAHONTAS DESCENDANTS:

3 Mary Bolling (1711-8/10/1744), m. 1/20/1727, Col. John Fleming
   (11/ /1697-11/6/1756)

But in SECOND CORRECTIONS AND ADDITIONS:

3 Mary Bolling, m. 1731 and died 1770. Her husband died 1766.

In THE SCOTS PEERAGE, Edited by Sir James Balfour Paul, Vol. 8,
   pages 548-550 (1907) (keyed to the descendants of John Fleming,
   first Earl of Wigton):

         John Fleming (1697-1756)
         Mary Bolling (ca. 1711-1744)

See also:
   FINDING YOUR FOREFATHERS IN AMERICA by A. F. Bennett. Chap.
   11, pages 123, 126, 128-33 (1957).

33152   Frank Devereaux Markham

331522   Frank Devereaux Markham, Jr.

331523122 Andrew Cody Burton (/ /1994-)
331523123 Mary Stephanie Burton (/ /1997-)

33152313   Jane Dubose Burton

331523141 Joseph Cooper Burton (/ /1993-)
331523142 Lucia Wright Burton (/ /1997-)

3315232   Frank Chapman Burton. Div. M. (3rd) 1991, Barbara
           Gillespie

331523313 Steven Daniel Conant (/ /1991-)
331523314 William Christian Conant (/ /1992-)
331523315 Carrie Elizabeth Conant (/ /1998-)

366 Thomas Bernard (-6/12/1833 or 6/11/1834), m. 12/29/
     1792, in Goochland Co., VA, Mary Hicks (d. in home of
     3661 in Clinton Co., OH). Her brother Meshack Hicks lived
     in Goochland Co. in 1847 and his wife was Ann Elizabeth
     _____. Her brother John Hicks and her sisters
     Nancy Hicks Carroll and Sally Hicks were living in 1847.
3661 Elizabeth ("Betsy") Bernard (ca. 1795-5/7/1861, age 66
     years, 6 mos., 17 days). (Bur. Westboro I.O.O.F.,
     Jefferson Township, Clinton Co., OH), m. 5/2/1822, (by
     Augustus Brown, J.P.) Francis Hayden Haddon Smithson (ca.
     1792 or 1796-after 1860) (b. in VA), son of Drummond and

Mary Parrott Smithson. In 1837-1840 family moved to Clinton Co. He was a farmer. Probably buried in same lot.

The 1860 census of Westboro, Jefferson Township, Clinton County, OH, shows:

Richard Bernard	age 24, b.o.
Mark Bernard	age 20, b.o.
Hattie Bernard	age 13, b.o.

36611   Mary Elizabeth Smithson (4/26/1824-11/15/1890) (died Chester, Wayne Co., IN, bur. Chester Cemetery) (also known as Mary Ann, shown as Mary Ellen on marriage record), m. 11/29/1849, in Clinton, OH, Milton L. Pickett (brother to Eli M.Pickett)

36612   Sarah Smithson (ca. 1825-   ), m. Peter Dennis

366121 Elizabeth Dennis (age 15 in 1860)

366122 Richard Dennis (age 12 in 1860) (twin)

366123 Frank Dennis (age 12 in 1860) (twin)

366124 Hannah Dennis (age 8 in 1860)

366125 Rose Dennis (age 3 in 1860)

36613   Martha A. Smithson (ca. 1825 in OH-   ), m. 9/15/1853, in Highland, OH (by Wm. J. Fee), Eli M. Pickett (brother to Milton L. Pickett)

36614   Elizabeth Smithson (ca. 1829-   ) (probably born in Highland Co., OH), m. 2/29/1856, in Clinton Co., Lynch Barber. She may have married first Elmore Jones.

36615   Susan E. Smithson (ca. 1832-   ) (probably born in Highland Co., OH), m. Stephen Fletcher

36616   Richard Thomas (or L.) Smithson (12/23/1826-5/18/1910) (probably born in Highland Co., OH, died in Alfalfa Co., OK. Bur. Good Hope Cemetery in Helena, OK), m. Martha Leonard (8/3/1838-5/8/1918) (b. in OH). Moved to OK in 1902. A farmer. Served in Co. H, 92nd Ohio Infantry. Disabled. Certificate: 965,826 Ohio.

366161 Julia Eva Smithson (1863-1946)

366162 William Francis Smithson (1865-1939) (b. in IL)

366163 John Wesley Smithson (age 11 in 1880) (b. in IL)

366164 Mary Jane ("Mollie") Smithson (age 9 in 1880) (b. in IL)

366165 Henry Almon Smithson (1876-1965) (b. in IL)

3664   George Washington Bernard (b. in Goochland Co.)

3665   Thomas Jefferson Bernard (-1/14/1867, age 64 years, 20 days). Probably buried in same lot as 3661.

3667   Susan (or Susana) Bernard (-1850), m. Samuel (or William) Rees (or Reese)

36676 William Rees

367   Richard Bernard (-1835 in Highland Co, OH), m. in 1798, in Rockbridge Co., VA, Mary Walker. Moved to Highland Co., OH, in 1805 and living there in 1820.

5111   John Bolling Eldridge, m. (2nd) 2/9/1852, Susannah
       Elizabeth Eddins (4/7/1834-ca. 1888), dau. of Benjamin
       Eddins (2/21/1794-7/2/1852) (b. SC - d. Madison Co., AL)
       and Mary Ann Clampitt (11/2/1807-11/7/1899) (b. TN -
       d. Madison Co. AL)

51115 Martha Ann Eldridge (ca. 1828-   ), m. Hugh L. Veal
       (Administrator of Elizabeth M. Eldridge's Estate,
       11/15/1853, Madison Co., AL)
51116 Mary Elizabeth Eldridge (ca. 1830-   ), m. 1847, John
       Bronaugh (ca. 1826-   ). Residing in Madison Co., AL,
       11/15/1853, when her mother's estate was settled.)
   Children by second wife:
51117 Robert S. Eldridge (ca. 1853-   )
51118 Margaret ("Maggie") Tabitha Diemer Eldridge (Diemer is
       the doctor who delivered her) (6/22/1855- / /1915)
       (b. Harvest, AL - d. Lincoln Co., TN, bur. Prosperity
       Cemetery, Yukon, TN), m. 9/17/1873, Lincoln Co., TN,
       William Joseph Hill (4/11/1838-7/23/1917), a Confederate
       Soldier, son of Ebenezer Hill, Jr. (printer) and Mary
       Tabitha Bryan Hill (sister of John Neely Bryan, first
       settler of Dallas)
511181 Kate Eldridge Hill (12/14/1874-   ) (b. Lincoln Co., TN
       - d. Michigan), m. 10/31/1895, Lincoln Co. TN, Aaron
       Rufus Goodenough of Lapeer, MI
5111811 Ethel May Goodenough (1/19/1897-   ) (b. Lincoln Co.,
       TN)
5111812 Mary Pearl Goodenough (11/29/1899-   ) (b. Lapeer, MI)
5111813 Raymond Lee Goodenough (9/24/1902-   ) (b. Lapeer, MI)
5111814 Adelbert Delyle Goodenough (8/27/1906-   ) (b. Lincoln
       Co., TN)
5111815 Chester Everett Goodenough (ca. 1908-   )
511182 Walter Vance Hill (7/6/1881-2/22/1959) (b. Lincoln Co.
       TN - d.Springdale, AR), m. (1st) 8/2/1903, Fayetteville,
       TN, Nellie Ethel Hall (1/12/1887-4/9/1917) (b. AL - d.
       Floydada, TX), dau. of Thomas Hall (a Union soldier)
       and Alpha Ann Bowers Hall; m. (2nd) 7/6/1940, Lubbock
       Co., TX, Hazel Ruth Pearson (1/17/1913-3/24/1996) (b.
       Wellington, TX - d. Springdale, AR), dau. of Walter
       and Eeva Pierce Pearson.
   Children by first wife:
5111821 William Henry Hill (7/10/1904-6/8/1966) (b. Fayette-
       ville, TN - d. Happy, TX, bur. Plainview, TX), m. (1st)
       8/ /1935, Jenny Belle; m. (2nd) 2/4/1939, Lubbock Co.,
       TX, Eunice Lydia Barton (1/20/1917-   ) (b. Concho
       Co., TX)
           Adopted child (son of Eunice Barton):
           Kenneth Eugene Hill (9/9/1936-   ) (b. Lubbock
           Co., TX), m. 8/20/1958, Hale Co., TX, Barbara Nell
           Fox (8/18/1940-   ) (b. Plainview, TX)
               i. Vance Lee Hill (1/23/1960-   ) (b. Barstow,
                   CA), m. 8/12/1978, Tammy Michelle Dalton

            1.   Jeremy John Hill (3/8/1979-   ) (b.
                  Hale Center, TX)
            2.   Rusty Vance Hill (5/23/1981-   ) (b.
                  Hale Center, TX)
      ii. David Eugene Hill (11/27/1960-   ) (b.
          Plainview, TX), m. 4/12/1986, Pamela Jean
          Junell
            1.   Jessica Proshea Hill (4/1/1987-   )
                  (b. Hale Center, TX)
            2.   Issac Fox Theodore Hill (1/8/1989-   )
                  (b. Hale Center, TX)
      iii. Roxanna Marie Hill (9/15/1965-   ) (b. Hale
          Center, TX), m. (1st) 1/17/1987, Raymond
          Diekl; m. (2nd) 10/1/1987, Charles Butch
          Hackler

51118211 Hulen Henry Hill (5/7/1940-   ) (b. Lubbock, TX), m.
          6/16/1967, Virginia Moudy (5/8/1945-   ) (b. Tulia,
          TX), dau. of Thomas Moudy
511182111 Tamaria Dawn Hill (2/26/1972-   )
51118212 Barbara Jean Hill (9/17/1942-   ) (b. Lubbock, TX), m.
          4/16/1961, Edwin Lee Nutt (2/28/1937-   ) (b. San
          Angelo, TX), son of Jewel and Ellie Turner Nutt
511182121 Daniel Lee Nutt (2/7/1962-   ) (b. Hale Center, TX),
          m. 6/30/1984, Fort Worth, TX, Laura Lee Pittman
          (1/26/1962-   ), dau. of Leonard and Carol Schultz
          Pittman
5111821211 Lindsey Lee Nutt (10/20/1985-   ) (b. Floydada, TX
5111821212 Jason Alan Nutt (12/24/1987-   ) (b. Floydada, TX
5111821213 Kaylie Leshay Nutt (3/19/1992-   ) (b. Lubbock, TX
511182122 Jeffery Mark Nutt (9/10/1963-   ) (b. Hale Center,
          TX), m. (1st) 7/24/1985, Floydada, TX, Karen Shuck,
          dau. of Bruce and Betty Shuck; m. (2nd) 8/7/1992,
          Floydada, TX, Loretta Turner (10/11/1970-   ), dau.
          of John and Mary Jones Turner
    Child by first wife:
5111821221 Seth Mark Nutt (9/24/1986-   ) (b. Floydada, TX)
    Children by second wife:
5111821222 Branson Skye Nutt (5/23/1993-   ) (b. Hale Center,
          TX)
5111821223 Taylor Lana'e Nutt (11/20/1995-   ) (b. Hale Center,
          TX)
511182123 Zachary Bill Nutt (12/2/1971-   ) (b. Hale Center,
          TX), m. 1/2/1993, Floydada, TX, Stacy Lanae Hinsley
          (7/3/1973-   ) (b. Lubbock, TX), dau. of Kim and
          Sarah Williams Hinsley
5111821231 Kelsey Jo Nutt (4/6/1995-   ) (b. Lubbock, TX)
5111821232 Corbin Michell Nutt (5/22/1997-   ) (b. Lubbock, TX)
51118213 Leroy Vance Hill (3/7/1944-   ) (b. Lubbock, TX), m.
          6/28/1986, Tulia, TX, Suella Edwards (8/15/1951-   )
511182131 Ethan Cole Hill (9/28/1989-   ) (b. Tulia, TX)
5111822 Robert E. Lee Hill (3/18/1907-6/27/1978) (b. Fayette-
          ville, TN - d. Lubbock, TX), m. 6/25/1927, Memphis,
          TX, Ethel Ida Walker (3/19/1910-2/26/1993), dau. of
          Oscar and Opie Walker

51118221   Robert E. Lee Hill, Jr. (6/25/1928-   ) (b. Clarendon,
           TX), m. 12/14/1951, Wolfforth, TX, Nelda June Griffis
           (1/21/1934-   )
511182211 Robert Michael Hill (7/15/1955-   ) (b. Lovington,
           NM), m. (1st) 4/7/1976, Sonja   ; m. (2nd)
           4/7/1989, Marie Corley McMillian (3/23/2958-   )
     Children by first wife:
5111822111 Michael Ross Hill (5/10/1977-   )
5111822112 Erica Lyn Hill (3/23/1980-   )
5111822113 Samantha Nicole Hill (9/16/1981-   )
     Stepchild:
           Sonie McMillian (4/13/1979-   )
511182212 Brian Mark Hill (8/17/1958-   ) (b. Levelland, TX),
           m. 6/16/1978, Susan Ranae Wright (2/5/1960-   )
5111822121 David Eric Hill (7/15/1980-   )
5111822122 Randi J'Lyn Hill (6/23/1983-   )
511182213 MeriLyn Hill (9/10/1963-   ) (b. Levelland, TX), m.
           5/22/1982, Barry Wayne Odell (1/13/1962-   )
5111822131 Kelsey Lyn Odell (4/9=8/1988-   )
51118222   Linda Janell Hill (12/13/1941-   ) (b. Lubbock, TX),
           m. 12/10/1965, Wolfforth, TX, Joe George Klattenhoff
           (12/13/1941-   ) (b. Lubbock, TX)
511182221 Kimberly Carol Klattenhoff (7/13/1967-7/13/1967)
     Adopted child:
           Christopher Edward Klattenhoff (9/24/1969-   ) (b.
           San antonio), m. 6/26/1993, Forth Worth, Angela Gale
           Boone
5111823   Eddie Margaret Hill (4/12/1909-9/19/1993) (b. Fayette-
           ville, TN - d. Commerce, TX, bur. Resthaven Cemetery,
           Lubbok, TX), m. 6/8/1927, Memphis, TX, Lacie Edward
           Tucker (1/22/1906-6/29/1990) (b. Glen Allen, AL -
           d. Lubbock, TX), son of Sherrod Demby and Dollie
           Jane Letson Tucker
51118231   Delmer Ray Tucker (2/26/1928-3/10/1928) (b. and d.
           Clarendon, TX, bur. Newlin Cemetery, Hall Co., TX)
51118232   Margie Faye Tucker (12/24/1934-   ) (b. Hurlwood,
           TX), m. (1st) 2/9/1952, Hurlwood, TX, Hival Franklin
           Forrester, son of Jesse and Frances Rollins Forrester;
           m. (2nd) 3/8/1963, Littlefield, TX, Thomas Stewart,
           Jr. (6/27/1933-   ) (b. Westerly, RI), son of Thomas
           and Olive Harris Stewart
511182321 Harlan Hival Forreter (7/15/1955-   ) (b. Lubbock,
           TX), m. (1st) 7/28/1978, Clarksville, TX, Katherine
           Susan Mills, dau. of Roger and Anita Pantel Mills;
           m. (2nd) 11/24/1988, Fresno, CA, Donna Diane Doering,
           dau. of Gerald and Elva Pendley Doering
     Children by first wife:
5111823211 Danita Brooke Forrester (12/26/1979-   ) (b. New
           Boston, TX)
5111823212 Candice Nicole Forrester (9/24/1981-   ) (b. Paris,
           TX)
5111823213 Sandra Erin Forrester (10/5/1983-   ) (b. Bonham, TX)

Children by second wife:
5111823214 Michael Lacie Forrester (11/19/1991-   ) (b. Porter-
            ville, CA)
5111823215 Kyle Dewayne Forrester (2/2/1993-   ) (b. Garland,
            TX)
511182322   Leatreca Diann Forrester (10/18/1956-6/20/1977) (b.
            Lubbock, TX - d. Weatherford, TX, in an automobile
            accident, two weeks before she was to be married)
51118233   Elner Leatrice Tucker (7/10/1941-   ) (b. Lubbock, TX),
            m. 12/21/1957, Hurlwood, TX, Bobby Glen Pettiet (3/3/
            1940-   ), son of Benjamin and Willie Hasty Pettiet
511182331   Michael Scott Pettiet (b. and d. 8/17/1960, Lubbock,
            TX, bur. Resthaven Cemetery, Lubbock, TX)
511182332   Dennis Todd Pettiet (8/17/1961-8/31/1961) (b. and d.
            Lubbock, TX, bur. Resthaven Cemetery, Lubbock, TX)
      Adopted children:
            i. Lisa Venita Michelle Pettiet (8/30/1962-   )
                (b. Fort Worth), m. 12/20/1984, Clarksville,
                TX, Joel Wayne Williams
                1. Whitney Elizabeth Williams (8/31/1991-   )
                    (b. Dallas)
                2. Natalie Christine Williams (9/5/1995-   )
                    (b. Dallas)
            ii. Bobby Scott Pettiet (11/9/1964-   ) (b. Fort
                Worth), m. 6/13/1987, Bogata, TX, Dusty Denise
                Damron
                1. Haley Nicole Pettiet (4/24/1995-   ) (b.
                    Lubbock, TX)
                2. Devon Scott Pettiet (2/26/1997-   ) (b.
                    Lubbock, TX)
5111824   Dessie Maude Hill (6/3/1912-8/13/1995) (b. Fayetteville,
          TN - d. Fresno, CA), m. 2/4/1932, Hollis, OK, Charles
          Russell Beasley, son of Garret and Marth McCloud
          Beasley
51118241   Martha Ann Beasley (11/5/1939-   ) (b. Lubbock, TX),
            m. (1st) 10/7/1953, Merced, CA, Gerald Ochoa Zapata,
            son of Manuel and Delores Ochoa Zapata; m. (2nd)
            6/10/1980, Reno, Dale Thomas Vandever
511182411   Roxana Lynn Zapata (1/9/1956-   ) (b. Fresno, CA), m.
            Randy Stephen Wymore, son of William Willington
            Wymore
5111824111 Montiana Adar Wymore (b. Fresno, CA)
5111824112 Nadia Raylena Wymore (b. Fresno, CA)
5111824113 Randy Wymore (b. Fresno, CA)
5111824114 William Willington Wymore (Jr.) (b. Fresno, CA)
5111824115 Rigel Tennyia Wymore (b. Fresno, CA)
511182412   Tanya Elaine Zapata (8/13/1959-   ) (b. Fresno, CA),
            m. (1st) Alex Lujan; m. (2nd) 1973, Faustino Calles
      Child by first husband:
5111824121 Juvan Lujan
      Children by second husband:
5111824122 Jairus Peter Calles
5111824123 Tiana Elice Calles

511182413   Sheryl Denise Zapata (3/7/1958-   ) (b. Fresno, CA),
        (1st) 4/ /1975, Tiajuana, Mexico, Trinidad M.
        Valenzuela; m. (2nd) 1994, Richard White
     Children by first husband:
5111824131 Dedan Jared Valenzuela (1/ /1976-   )
5111824132 Trinidad M. Valenzuela, Jr., m. Debra _____

51118241321 Desarie Monique Valenzuela
51118241322 Annette Renae Valenzuela (6/7/1995-   )
5111824133 Danae Danielle Valenzuela
5111824134 Tarrin Valenzuela
     Child by second husband:
5111824135 Alexis Ricki White (6/12/1995-   )
51118242   Charles Lester Beasley (6/29/1935-   ) (b. Bakersville,
        CA), m. Los Angles, Patricia Padget, dau. of Frederick
        and Mildred Padget
511182421 Andrea Elice Beasley, m. Mark Johnson of Los Angeles
511182422 Charles Russell Beasley (b. Los Angeles)
511182423 Randell Vincent Beasley (b. Reno)
51118243   Harlan Henry Beasley (4/8/1937-   ) (b. Lubbock, TX),
        m. (1st) 11/15/1958, Yuma, AZ, Brenda Mariah Sylvia;
        m. (2nd) 1989, Graciela Olivia Mejie Rivera, dau. of
        Mariano and Juventina Mejia Rivera
     Children by first wife:
511182431 Sabrina Gay Beasley (8/28/1959-   ) (b. Lancaster,
        CA), m. (1st) in Porterville, CA, Randy Richey; m.
        (2nd) Mark Crumb
     Children by first wife:
5111824311 Brandy Richey (/ /1980-   )
5111824312 Sarah Richey (/ /1982-   )
511182432 Scott Anthony Beasley (8/1/1964-   ) (b. Las Vegas),
        m. (1st) 1982, Las Vegas, Jamie Zigler; m. (2nd)
        1994, Yorba Linda, CA, Lisa Marie Figaroa
     Child by first wife:
5111824321 Tarrar Beasley (10/15/1987-   ) (b. Orange, CA)
     Child by second wife:
5111824322 Scott Anthony Beasley, Jr. (12/31/1996-   ) (b.
        Denver)
     Child by second wife:
511182433 Hondo Harlan Beasley (4/11/1991-   ) (b. Anahiem, CA)
     Stepchild:
        Dinia Mirbell Orrellana (10/10/1988-   ) (b. Elprogresso,
        Honoduras)
51118244   Joyce Yvonne Beasley (12/24/1940-   ) (b. Bakersfield,
        CA), m. (1st) Las Vegas, Andrew Gomez; m. (2nd)
        William Solven
511182441 Robin Andrew Gomez, m. Jennifer Jayne, dau. of Curtis
        and Rita Ripple Jayne
5111824411 Maximillion Austin Gomez (10/ /1991-   ) (b. Fresno,
        CA
5111825   Nellie Ethel Hill (4/8/1917-3/11/1986) (b. Floydada, TX
        - d. Wilberton, OK; bur. Veteran Colony Cemetery), m.
        (1st) 12/26/1938, Clovis, NM, William Lace ("Skinny")
        Allford; m. (2nd) 1975, Lubbock, TX, Omer Bunion Duncan

Adopted children by first husband:
   i. Judith Lorraine Allford (5/20/1948-   ) (b. French
       Camp, CA), m. 5/15/1968, Lubbock, TX, Glen Aubrey
       Bell
       1. Bryan Aubrey Bell (3/4/1980-   )
       Adopted child:
       2. Sheila Gay Bell (7/10/1970-   ) (b. Lubbock,
           TX), m. 6/6/1991, Darren Duvall
             Jessica Shean Duvall (4/16/1991-   ) (b.
               McAlester, OK)
             Jerry Shane Duvall (4/13/1993-   ) (b.
               Muskogee, OK)
  ii. Shirley Ann Allford (5/12/1949-   ) (b. Racine,
       WI), m. (1st) James Wayne Boone; m. (2nd) 2/14/
       1967, Mark Wayne Ross; m. (3rd) 5/28/1989, Reno,
       William Henry Hood
       1. Marcella DeAnn Ross (7/30/1967-   ) (b.
           Lubbock, TX), m. 9/2/1983, David Berry Owens;
           m. (2nd) 6/2/1988, Stephen Kelly Frazier
           Children by first huband:
           Benjamin Lee Owens (5/28/1984-   ) (b.
             McAlester, OK)
           Somner Cheri Owens (1/14/1987-   ) (b.
             Brunsville, MN)
           Children by second husband:
           Felicia Maria Frazier (3/20/1989-   ) (b.
             St. Paul)
           Jeremiah John Frazier (7/20/1991-   ) (b.
             Brunsville MN)
       2. Marllena LeAnn Ross (8/4/1968-   ) (b.
           Minneapolis)
Children by second wife:
5111826 Eva Sue Hill (7/13/1941-   ) (b. Lubbock, TX), m. 10/3/
      1959, Eureka Springs, AR, Louie Edwin Benn (1/18/2934-
) (b. Springvalley, AR), son of Ila Marie Benn
51118261 Edwin Everett Benn (5/1/1960-   ) (b. Siloam Springs,
      AR), m. 9/22/1985, Fayetteville, AR, Brenda Sue
      Milligan (12/8/1959-   ), dau. of James E. and Norma
      Laringham Milligan
511182611 Jason Everett Benn (4/12/1986-   ) (b. Fayetteville,
       AR)
511182612 Katherine Olivia Benn (10/10/1993-   ) (b. Fayette-
       ville, AR)
    Adopted child (son of Brenda Milligan)
       Joshua Cory Bemn (2/8/1981-   ) (b. Fayetteville, AR)
51118262 George Russell Benn (3/9/1964-   ) (b. Siloam Springs,
      AR)
51118263 Kenneth Jerred Benn (6/20/1967-   ) (b. Springdale,
      AR), m. 6/17/1995, Fayetteville, AR, Patricia Dawn
      Usrey, dau. of Cleston Brannon and Charlene Taylor
511182631 Nicholas Jerred Benn (3/31/1998-   ) (b. Springdale,
       AR)

Stepchild:
        Payton Allan Usrey (11/17/1989-   ) (b. Springdale,
        AR)
5111827 Mary Valieth Hill (7/28/1942-   ) (b. Lubbock, TX), m.
        6/7/1963, Springdale, AR, Ralph Eugene Scott (12/24/
        1938-   ), son of Pierce and Eunice Prince Scott
51118271 Douglas Eugene Scott (7/21/1969-   ) (b. Springdale,
        AR), m. 5/15/1993, Springdale, AR, Kristin Renee
        Browning, dau. of Sid and Linda Browning
511182711 Tyler Douglas Scott (6/28/1994-   ) (b. Stockton, CA)
511182712 Emma Renee Scott (3/29/1997-   ) (b. Stockton, CA)
511183 Maggie Sue Hill (4/6/1887-   ) (b. Lincoln Co., TN - d.
        Dallas), m. 10/13/1904, Fayetteville, TN, John Isaac
        Williams
5111831 Oscar Raymond Williams (8/8/1905-   ) (b. Lincoln Co.,
        TN - d. Dallas), m. Luena McBee
5111832 Herbert Howard Williams (11/21/1907-4/5/1908) (b. and d.
        Lincoln Co., TN)
5111833 Walter Lee Williams (2/24/1908-   ) (b. Lincoln Co, TN.
        - d. Dallas), m. Lula Smitty
5111834 Ruthie Mae Williams (6/23/1912-   ) (b. and d. Dallas),
        m. Jess Key
51118341 Gerald Wayne Key
51118342 Edith Maxine Key
5111835 Ruby Clare Williams (11/2/1916-   ) (b. and d. Dallas),
        m. Frank Cole
51118351 Louise Cole, m. Charles Womack
51118352 Margaret Ruth Cole
51118353 Frankie Cole
5111836 Opal Gladys Williams (5/27/1921-   ) (b. and d. Dallas),
        m. James Key
51118361 Linda Key, m. Russell Milsap
51118362 Melba Key
51118363 Laura Ann Key
5111837 Lester Erskin Williams (8/27/1924-   ) (b. and d.
        Dallas), m. Blanch Wasivich
51118371 Barbara Elaine Williams
51118372 Robert A. Williams
51118373 Carolyn Sue Williams
51118374 Raymond Williams
5111838 Estol Wayne Williams (4/10/1927-   ) (b. and d. Dallas)
511184 Oscar Julian Hill (5/23/1994-   ) (b. TN - d. Chatta-
        nooga), m. Nova Layton
5111841 Layton Hill
5111842 Thomas Hill
5111843 Julian Hill
511185 William Earnest Hill (2/7/1899-2/11/1899) (b. and d.
        Lincoln Co., TN, bur. Prosperity Cemetery, Yukon, TN)
51119   Simen A. Eldridge (ca. 1859-   ) (b. Al - d. TX), m.
        4/12/1876, Madison Co., AL, Andrew J. McClain, son of
        J. A. McClain
511191 Fortince McClain (ca. 1878-   ) (b. and d. TX)

55231   Virginia Bell Pankey (b. Manchester, VA, 6/11/1822-
         7/19/1852), m. 2/10/1847, Joseph Pendleton Winston
         (4/5/1825-7/3/1880). He later had a second wife.

552312   Charles Pankey Winston (b. Richmond, 1/22/1848-1/1/1887),
         m. Caroline ("Carrie") Scott Gay (4164)
5523121   Mary A. Winston
5523122   Richard P. Winston (2/26/1880-   ). Home: Richmond
5523123   Cary Gay Winston
5523124   Virginia Bell Winston

564211   John Adolphus Mahon, m. Ethel Pauline Jacobs, dau. of
         James Simeon and Jane Pickens Felder Jacobs. Ethel bur.
         in Mobile. John may have been born in Mobile.
5642111   Marie Clayton Mahon (b. Meridian, MS), m. George Clark
         Marlette, M.D., of Haynesville, AL
56421111   Sarah Janice Marlette, m. Cyril Busing Burch, M.D.
564211111   Martha Elizabeth Burch
564211112   Cyril Busing ("Buz") Burch, Jr.
564211113   Katharine Augusta Burch
56421112   Ethel Pauline Marlette (8/27/1926-   ), m. 1/22/1949,
         Charles Frederick Anepohl, Jr.
564211121   Charles ("Chuck") Frederick Anepohl III (12/4/1950-
                ), m. Joan Gay Jarvis
5642111211   Charles Frederick Anepohl IV (11/6/1982-   )
5642111212   Melissa Lauren Anepohl (12/25/1983-   )
564211122   Gay Clark Anepohl, m. (1st) 5/26/1984, Paul Eric
         Jersak (-12/2/1986), m. (2nd) 10/8/1990,
         William Max Yarbrough
5642111221   Sarah Ann Yarbrough (9/14/1993-   )

5642112   Susie Mahon
5642113   Gertrude Agnes Mahon

564212   Ethel Walker Mahon (11/27/1907-   )
564213   John Adolphus Mahon, Jr. (10/3/1911-   )

64   Margaret ("Peggy") Murray, m. Thomas Gordon (1744-   ) who,
     prior to 1763, came from Galloway, and was a merchant and
     a member of the Petersburg firm of Westmore, Gordon and
     Murray. They lived at "Blandford". He was a vestryman
     of Bristol Parish. His second wife was the widow Elizabeth
     Baird Westmore.
641 Anne ("Nancy") Gordon (b. 7/13/1776-   ). Bur. "Woodlawn".
     M. Col. Henry Embry Coleman, a juror in the 1807 trial of
     Aaron Burr and a Colonel in the War of 1812. Inherited
     "Woodlawn" and is bur. there. Son of Mary Embry Coleman.
6411 Elizabeth Anne Coleman (1797-8/10/1821), m. Charles
     Baskerville, born in Mecklenburg County, the eldest son
     of his parents of "Lombardy Grove". He attended the
     University of Edinburgh and his portrait was painted by
     Sir Henry Raeburn. Bur. "Lombardy Grove". Elizabeth
     Anne Coleman died at birth of fourth child and bur.
     "Lombardy Grove".
64111 Col. William Baskerville, m. Susanna Riddick Jiggetts (d.
     1860), dau. of David E. and Susanna Bullock Jiggetts of
     Mecklenburg County. After the Civil War "Buena Vista"
     was sold and the Baskervilles moved to "Eagle Point",
     near Clarksville.

641113 Charles Baskerville, m., in Fall of 1864, Alice Merle
     Sampson (1846-1924), dau. of Rev. Francis S. and
     Caroline Dudley Sampson, the eldest of ten children.
     Charles Baskerville left Hampden Sydney College at
     the beginning of the Civil War and became a Second
     Lieutenant of the 1st Battalion of the Virginia
     Infantry and was promoted in 1864. Settled in Prince
     Edward County and raised thoroughbred horses at Hampden
     Sydney.

641113111   Charles Baskerville Saunders, Jr., m. Margaret
            MacIntire Shafer (1927-   )
6411131111 Charles Baskerville Saunders III, m. Mary Cornell Rus
            (1953-   )

6411131112 George Carlton Saunders, m. Cyntia Matossian (1954-
)
64111311121 Nora Matossian Saunders
6411131113 Margaret Keyser Saunders, m. Stephen David Spector
            (1953-   )
64111311131 Julian Saunders Spector
64111311132 Cary Saunders Spector
6411131114 Lucy Carmichael Saunders, m. Glenn Paul Kish (1955-
)

6411131115 John Rolfe Saunders (1961-   ), m. Roberta Christine
            Reed (1962-   ). Div. 1998.

641113112   Susie Baskerville Saunders, m. John Francis McClatchey
            (1929-   )

6411131122   Mary Spottswood McClatchey, m. Stephen Girard
    Masciocchi (1958-)
64111311221 Julian Anthony Masciocchi (1999-)

641113113 Ashby Carmichael Saunders, m. Mary Virginia Swain
    (1933-)
6411131131 Charles Spencer Saunders, m. Amy Clinton Heffner
    (1965-)
64111311311 Aubrey Peirce Saunders (1999-)

64111311313 Susannah Baskerville Saunders, m. David George
    Roberts (1966-)
641113113131 Kyle David Roberts (1997-)

Virginia Legends

   A Pocahontas granite plaque giving her brief biography
and a similar plaque for Captain John Smith are among the twenty-
four included in Virginia Legends, a walk in Virginia Beach,
Virginia.

Index

NOTE: The name of the spouse of a Pocahontas descendant is indexed even though that spouse is not a descendant of Pocahontas, but the name of a parent of such a spouse is not indexed unless, of course, that parent is a descendant of Pocahontas.

Bolling, Alexander 13444a1
Bolling, Alexander Moseley 13444a
Bolling, Amanda E. Harris 13444
Bolling, Amanda Elizabeth 134445
Bolling, Bonni Van Fleet 13444b21
Bolling, Brandon Lee 13444b332
Bolling, Callie Williams 13444a
Bolling, Douglas William 13444b333
Bolling, Elizabeth Snoddy 13444b3
Bolling, Florence Eveline 134447
Bolling, Frances P. _____ 1344
Bolling, Holly Sue 13444b211
Bolling, Irma Richardson 13444b2
Bolling, Ivanhoe Alfonso 13444b
Bolling, Jessie Lee Keys 13444b33
Bolling, Joan Elizabeth 13444b31
Bolling, Julian 13444x
Bolling, Lenaeus, M.D. 13444
Bolling, Lenaeus 134446
Bolling, Lenaeus, Jr. 1345
Bolling, Louisanna Steptoe 134448
Bolling, Mary 3
Bolling, Mary Amanda 13444b1
Bolling, Mary Eleanor 134443
Bolling, Mary Jane 13444b32
Bolling, Mary Pearl Payne 13444b
Bolling, Nathan Leneas 13444b2
Bolling, Nell 13444b4
Bolling, Philip Augustus 134444
Bolling, Philip Ivanhoe 13444b21
Bolling, Pocahontas 13441
Bolling, Powhatan, 135
Bolling, Rena 13444a2
Bolling, Robert, Jr. 13443
Bolling, Robert Glover 13444b3
Bolling, Robert Glover, Jr. 13444b33
Bolling, Robert Langhorn 134442
Bolling, Robert Markham 1344
Bolling, Robert Shawn 13444b331
Bolling, Sarah Pocahontas 134441
Bolling, Susan Peyton 13442
Bolling, Virginia _____ 13444a1
Bolling, Virginia Argyle Harrison ("Pinkie")
  134449
Booth, Alexander Galt 242445221
Booth, Emily Tryon Hoge 242445221
Booth, Julia Mengel 2424452211
Bosworth, Stephanie 1326265225
Boutwell, Vicki Love 1322133414
Brace, Jeffrey Alan 13221334111
Brace, Jessica Polk 13221334112
Brace, Sallie Moore Benson 1322133411
Brace, Thomas Alan 1422133411
Breen, Judith Ellen 2424452411
Bronaugh, John 51116
Bronaugh, Mary Elizabeth Eldridge 51116
Brown, _____ 13442121
Brown, Lois Mann 13442121
Browning, Kristin Renee 51118271
Bruns, Alan Martin 21221422
Bruns, Bryan Randolph 212214221
Bruns, Jean Graham Randolph 21221422
Bruns, Lily Busaba 2122142211
Bruns, Mary Anderson 212214222
Bruns, Papking Chalad Daun Ngeun 212214221
Bruns, Robin Chalad 2122142212
Buhl, Jeremy Jay 24244524121

Buhl, Sarah Britton Hoge 24244524121
Burch, Cyril Busing 56421111
Burch, Cyril Busing ("Buz"), Jr. 564211112
Burch, Katharine Augusta 564211113
Burch, Martha Elizabeth 564211111
Burch, Sarah Janice Marlette 56421111
Burgess, Angel Marie 24142x113242
Burgess, Bali Nicole 24142x113261
Burgess, Chaylor Blaine 24142x113271
Burgess, Christina Rachelle 24142x113251
Burgess, Evelyn Joyce 24142x11321
Burgess, John Austin 24142x113262
Burgess, Joshua Dean 24142x113252
Burgess, Kathleen Rochelle 24142x11323
Burgess, Larisa Jane 24142x11326
Burgess, Lisa Grace 224142x11327
Burgess, Lisette Marie Rodrigue 24142x11325
Burgess, Marilyn Rene 24142x11322
Burgess, Susan Jane 24142x11324
Burgess, Susan Jane 24142x113243
Burgess, Susan Jane Lancaster 24142x1132
Burgess, Thomas 24142x1132
Burgess, Thomas, Jr. 24142x11325
Burgess, Thomas III 24142x113253
Burgess, Thomas Walter 24142x113241
Burks, Edith 1344218
Burnett, Elizabeth Blake 24244525122
Burnett, Miranda Blake Schuler 2424452512
Burnett, Sigrid Anne Croft 24244525121
Burnett, William Brown 2424452512
Burnett, William Brown, Jr. 24244525121
Burton, Andrew Cody 331523122
Burton, Barbara Gillespie 3315232
Burton, Frank Chapman 3315232
Burton, Jane Dubose 33152313
Burton, Joseph Cooper 331523141
Burton, Lucia Wright 331523142
Burton, Mary Stephanie 331523123
Burton, Patricia 2424452422
Butler, Jane Kean Randolph 24142x113

-C-

Cain, Jean 13444935
Caldwell, Frances Archer 251631131
Caldwell, Jessie Samantha 2516311313
Caldwell, Louisa Archer 2516311312
Caldwell, Mason Blake III 251631131
Caldwell, Mason Blake IV 2516311311
Calles, Faustino 511182412
Calles, Jairus Peter 5111824122
Calles, Tanya Elaine Zapata Lujan 511182412
Calles, Tiana Elice 5111825123
Campbell, Elizabeth Tinsley 24244522
Case, James 132626531
Case, Ruth Ann Schneider 132626531
Casoria, Darrell 13444b111
Casoria, Lorraine Simard 13444b11
Casoria, Simon 13444b11
Casoria, Simon (Jr.) 13444b112
Catlett, Myrtle Maude 134421
Childress, Katherine Lee 1344491
Cobb, _____ (twin of 134421-John Robert
  Cobb) 134422
Cobb, Barbara Ann 13442114
Cobb, Blanche 1344213
Cobb, Bolling Alfred 1344218

Cobb, Brenda Gayle 13442181
Cobb, David Glenn 134421111
Cobb, Edith Burks 1344218
Cobb, Eloise Hockaday 13442113
Cobb, Frances 1344212
Cobb, Frances Downey 1344216
Cobb, Frances Maxine 13442112
Cobb, George LeGarrel ("Gary") 1344211
Cobb, George LeGarrel, Jr. 13442111
Cobb, Ida Davis 1344211
Cobb, Jason Michael 134421821
Cobb, Jean C._____ 1344215
Cobb, John Oliver 1344216
Cobb, John Robert 134421
Cobb, John Robert 13442113
Cobb, Lisa 13442152
Cobb, Michael Robert 13442182
Cobb, Olive 1344217
Cobb, Rebecca ("Becky") Hammack 13442111
Cobb, Rickey Lynn 13442183
Cobb, Ruth 1344214
Cobb, Tracy Renee 134421112
Cobb, Vicky Cyrus 13442182
Cobb, Wylie Hubbard 1344215
Cobb, Wylie Hubbard, Jr. 13442151
Cobbs, Henry LeGare 13442
Cobbs, John Robert 134421
Cobbs, Myrtle Maude Catlett 134421
Cobbs, Susan Peyton Bolling 13442
Colden, Curtis Stephen 222312111
Colden, Nancy Randolph Gunn 222312111
Cole, Frank 5111835
Cole, Frankie 51118353
Cole, Louise 51118351
Cole, Margaret Ruth 51118352
Cole, Ruby Clare Williams 5111835
Coleman, Anne ("Nancy") Gordon 641
Coleman, Elizabeth Anne 6411
Coleman, Col. Henry Embry 641
Conant, Carrie Elizabeth 331523315
Conant, Steven Daniel 331523313
Conant, William Christian 331523314
Connell, Chandra Faith 2421545222
Connoll, Debra 2424452423
Cook, Bobby Houston 13442143
Cook, Gordon Terry 13442141
Cook, Harvey 1344214
Cook, Jesse Norman 13442142
Cook, Ruth Cobb 1344214
Cooke, Donald Davis 2424452211
Cooke, Julia Mengel Booth 2424452211
Cookson, Theresa ("Terri") 2424452411
Craig, Katherine Elizabeth 2424452653
Croft, Sigrid Anne 24244525121
Crotty, Anne Holladay 2424452342
Crotty, Arthur Paul 2424452234
Crotty, Dorothy Holladay Hoge 2424452234
Crotty, Robert William 24244522341
Crumb, Mark 511182431
Crumb, Sabrina Gay Beasley Richey 511182431
Cyrus, Vicky 13442182

-D-

Daugherty, Doris Dee 2424452412
Davis, Clarence 1344217
Davis, Ida 1344211

Davis, Olive Cobb 1344217
Dehn, Gabrille 212214212
Dennis, Elizabeth 366121
Dennis, Frank 366123
Dennis, Hannah 366124
Dennis, Peter 36612
Dennis, Richard 366122
Dennis, Rose 366125
Dennis, Sarah Smithson 36612
Dobson, Parrish Cummings 242445231
Doering, Donna Diane 511182321
Dowdy, Richard B. 13442
Dowdy, Susan Peyton Bolling Cobbs 13442
Downey, Frances 1344216
Duncan, Nellie Ethel Hill Allford 5111825
Duncan, Omer Bunion 5111825
Durham, James 13262633
Durham, Mary Lou Holloway 13262633
Dwyer, Grace Ashley 242445232213
Dwyer, Ian 24244523221
Dwyer, Noel Luise Houston 24244523221
Dwyer, Sarah Luise 242445232212
Dwyer, William Jackson ("Jack") 24244523221

-E-

Eddins, Susannah Elizabeth 5111
Edwards, Suella 51118213
Eldridge, John Bolling 5111
Eldridge, Margaret ("Maggie") Tabitha
  Diemer 51118
Eldridge, Martha Ann 51115
Eldridge, Mary Elizabeth 51116
Eldridge, Robert S. 51117
Eldridge, Simen A. 51119
Eldridge, Susannah Elizabeth Eddins 5111
Ely, Lynn Luise 2424452322
Emerson, George Waldo 2424452111
Emerson, George Waldo, Jr. 24244521112
Emerson, Mary Randolph 24244521111
Emerson, Mary Stuart ("Stuey") Anderson
  2424452111
Estrada, Jose Gullero 212214211
Estrada, Mary Sommers Knight 212214211
Estrada, Noel Josefino 2122142111
Estrada, William Gustavo 212214212
Evarts, Alexandra M. 242453b1142
Evarts, Darragh Patricia 242453b1152
Evarts, Emily McFadden 24243b113
Evarts, Harrison William 242453b1151
Evarts, Jane Randolph 242453b112
Evarts, John Randolph Harrison 242453b115
Evarts, Kathleen Kearns 242453b115
Evarts, Mariah Stanard 242453b1112
Evarts, Remi J. 242453b1143
Evarts, Sophie M. 242453b1141
Evarts, Susanna Dashiel 24245b1113
Evarts, Thomas W. M. 242453b114

-F-

Farrar, Dorothy Virginia Genau 242154511
Farrar, Douglas Patch 2421545113
Farrar, Emily Summerville 24215451113
Farrar, Frederick Lyon 2421545112
Farrar, Ilan William 2421545115
Farrar, Jessie Bel Summerville 2421545111

Farrar, Col. John Henderson, Jr. 242154511
Farrar, John Henderson III 2421545111
Farrar, John Summerville 24215451111
Farrar, Karen Sue Rice 2421545112
Farrar, Leah Summerville 24215451112
Farrar, Magen Rice 24215451121
Farrar, Olivia Summerville 24215451114
Farrar, Sharon Mabel 2421545116
Farrar, Tamar Agmon 242154511
Farrar, Virginia Lee 2421545114
Farrar, Virginia Martinisi-Moglia 2321545113
Farwell, Edith ("Edie") 2424452651
Farwell, Susan Day 2424452323
Fielden, Dorothy ("Dolly") Cromwell
                                    242445232
Figaroa, Lisa Marie 511182432
Findley, Bill 13444b4
Findley, Cleo Patricia 13444b41
Findley, Nell Bolling 13444b4
Fleming, Col. John 3
Fleming, Mary Bolling 3
Fletcher, Stephen 36615
Fletcher, Susan E. Smithson 36615
Ford, Addison B. 134441
Ford, Sarah Pocahontas Bolling 134441
Forrester, Candice Nicole 5111823212
Forrester, Danita Brooke 5111823211
Forrester, Donna Diane Doering 511182321
Forrester, Harlan Hival 511182321
Forrester, Hival Franklin 51118232
Forrester, Katherine Susan Mills 511182321
Forrester, Kyle Dewayne 5111823215
Forrester, Leatreca Diann 511182322
Forrester, Margie Faye Tucker 51118232
Forrester, Michael Lacie 5111823214
Forrester, Sandra Erin 5111823213
Fox, Alexander Mead 2424452321
Fox, David 2424452632
Fox, Merrill Fowler Mead 2424452632
Fox, Nicholas Peyton Mead 24244526322
Freeman, Cleo Patricia Findley 13444b41
Freeman, Steve 13444b41

-G-

Gaffney, John Patrick, Jr. 24142x11326
Gattemeier, Larisa Jane Burgess 24142x11326
Gattemeier, Barbara Ruth Jackson 132626511
Gattemeier, Pete 132626511
Gay, Caroline ("Carrie") Scott 552312
Genau, Dorothy Virginia 242154511
Gerhart, Elizabeth Ann 24244524151
Gerhart, Margaret Knight Hoge 2424452415
Gerhart, Robert Willis, Jr. 2424452415
Gerhart, Virginia Buchanan 24244524152
Gillespie, Barbara 3315232
Gomez, Andrew 51118244
Gomez, Jennifer Jayne 511182441
Gomez, Joyce Yvonne Beasley 51118244
Gomez, Maximillion Austin 5111824411
Gomez, Robin Andrew 511182441
Goodenough, Aaron Rufus 511181
Goodenough, Adelbert Delyle 5111814
Goodenough, Chester Everett 5111815
Goodenough, Ethel May 5111811
Goodenough, Kate Eldridge Hill 511181
Goodenough, Mary Pearl 5111812
Goodenough, Raymond Lee 5111813
Gordon, Anne ("Nancy") 641

Gordon, Margaret ("Peggy") Murray 64
Gordon, Thomas 64
Grazier, James 132626532
Grazier, Linda Lee Schneider 132626532
Griffis, Nelda June 51118221
Griffith, Augustus Reeves 111326541
Griffith, Elizabeth Graham Hassell 111326541
Gunn, Elizabeth Purnell 222312112
Gunn, James Steirling 22231211
Gunn, Margaret Woodson Barnhart 22231211
Gunn, Nancy Randolph 222312111
Gunnels, Brandon 24244526333
Gunnels, Caroline Jackson Mead 2424452633
Gunnels, Jennifer 24244526332
Gunnels, Laura 24244526331
Gunnels, Marc 2424452633

-H-

Hageman, Elizabeth ("Libba") Knight Hoge
                                    2424452413
Hageman, James Hoge 24244524132
Hageman, Richard Bernard, Jr. 2424452413
Hageman, Richard Bernard III 24244524131
Hall, Amanda Katherine 134449331
Hall, Amanda Virginia Payne 13444933
Hall, Conrad Livingston 13444933
Hall, Mildred Anne 134449333
Hall, Nellie Ethel 511182
Hall, Steven Jackson 134449332
Hammack, Rebecca ("Becky") 13442111
Harmon, Elizabeth ("Sabine") 2424452652
Harris, Amanda E. 13444
Harris, Elizabeth Ann 242445241
Harrison, Michael David 2424173921
Harrison, Virginia Randolph ("Mere")
                                    242445
Hassell, Elizabeth Graham 111326541
Hassell, Jane Mathis 111326542
Hawkins, Katherine Anne 1344493332
Hawkins, Margaret Amanda 134449331
Hawkins, Mildred Anne Hall 134449333
Hawkins, Philip Edward 134449333
Heffner, Amy Clinton 64111311331
Helm, Alexander Veasy 24244524222
Helm, Ben 24244524223
Helm, Charles 24244524232
Helm, Debra Connoll 2424452423
Helm, Elizabeth Jennifer Schmick 2424452421
Helm, Hunt Choteau 2424452423
Helm, Kay Stewart 2424452423
Helm, Mary Emily Mitchell 24244524212
Helm, Nell Hunt Hoge 242445242
Helm, Patricia Burton 2424452422
Helm, Peyton Randolph 2424452422
Helm, Randolph Burton 24244524221
Helm, Thomas Kennedy, Jr. 242445242
Helm, Thomas Kennedy III 2424452421
Helm, Thomas Kennedy IV 24244524211
Herrick, Laura Rebecca 2424452222
Hettrick, Pamella Bartlett 2424452221
Hicks, Mary 366
Hill, Barbara Jean 51118212
Hill, Brian Mark 511182212
Hill, Caroline 2424452231
Hill, David Eric 5111822121
Hill, Dessie Maude 5111824
Hill, Eddie Margaret 5111823

Hill, Erica Lyn 5111822112
Hill, Ethan Cole 511182131
Hill, Ethel Ida Walker 5111822
Hill, Eunice Lydia Barton 5111821
Hill, Eva Sue 5111826
Hill, Hazel Ruth Pearson 511182
Hill, Hulen Henry 51118211
Hill, Jenny Belle 5111821
Hill, Julian 5111843
Hill, Kate Eldridge 511181
Hill, Layton 5111841
Hill, Leroy Vance 51118213
Hill, Linda Janell 51118222
Hill, Maggie Sue 511183
Hill, Margaret ("Maggie") Tabitha Diemer
   Eldridge 51118
Hill, Marie Corley McMillian 511182211
Hill, Mary Valieth 5111827
Hill, MeriLyn 511182213
Hill, Michael Ross 5111822111
Hill, Nelda June Griffis 51118221
Hill, Nellie Ethel 5111825
Hill, Nellie Ethel Hall 511182
Hill, Nova Layton 511184
Hill, Oscar Julian 511184
Hill, Randi J'Lyn 5111822122
Hill, Robert E. Lee 5111822
Hill, Robert E. Lee, Jr. 51118221
Hill, Robert Michael 511182211
Hill, Samantha Nicole 5111822113
Hill, Suella Edwards 51118213
Hill, Susan Ranae Wright 511182212
Hill, Tamaria Dawn 511182111
Hill, Thomas 5111842
Hill, Virginia Moudy 51118211
Hill, Walter Vance 511182
Hill, William Earnest 511185
Hill, William Henry 5111821
Hill, William Joseph 51118
Hinsley, Stacy Lanae 511182123
Hockaday, Eloise 13442113
Hockaday, Gary 134421131
Hockaday, Robert Thomas 134421132
Hof, Brenda Gayle Cobb Reynolds Mitchell
   13442181
Hof, Fredic C. 13442181
Hoge, Alexandra Anne 24244522311
Hoge, Amanthis Bullitt 24244524111
Hoge, Anne Holladay 2424452232
Hoge, Blanche Smith 2424452414
Hoge, Blanche Weissinger Smith 24244524
Hoge, Caroline Hill 2424452231
Hoge, Cary Evelyn 24244526
Hoge, Catherine Carlisle 24244524122
Hoge, Doris Dee Daugherty 2424452412
Hoge, Dorothy Dean O'Brien 242445223
Hoge, Dorothy Holladay 2424452234
Hoge, Edith Louise ("Jonnie") Johnson
   Vatter 242445223
Hoge, Elizabeth Addison 24244525
Hoge, Elizabeth Ann Harris 242445241
Hoge, Elizabeth ("Libba") Knight 2424452413
Hoge, Elizabeth Tinsley Campbell 24244522
Hoge, Emily Tryon 242445221
Hoge, Emily Tryon Mengel 24244522
Hoge, George Stuart 24244524123
Hoge, George Weissinger Smith 2424452412
Hoge, Jane Lacy 2424452235

Hoge, Judith Ellen Green 2424452411
Hoge, Margaret Knight 2424452415
Hoge, Mary Holladay 242445222
Hoge, Mary O'Brien 2424452233
Hoge, Mary Stuart 24244523
Hoge, Mary Stuart Holladay 2424452
Hoge, Nell Hunt 242445242
Hoge, Rev. Peyton Harrison Hoge 2424452
Hoge, Peyton Harrison, Jr. 24244524
Hoge, Peyton Harrison III 242445241
Hoge, Peyton ("Peyho") Harrison IV
   2424452411
Hoge, Peyton Harrison V 24244524
Hoge, Sarah Britton 24244524121
Hoge, Theresa ("Terri") Cookson 2424452411
Hoge, Virginia Randolph Bolling 24244521
Hoge, Virginia Randolph ("Mere") Harrison
   242445
Hoge, Rev. William James 242445
Hoge, William Lacy 24244522
Hoge, William Lacy, Jr. 242445223
Hoge, William Lacy III 2424452231
Holladay, Mary Stuart 2424452
Holloway, Harry 1326263
Holloway, Harry, Jr. 13262631
Holloway, Joseph 13262632
Holloway, Mary Lou 13262633
Holloway, Mary Mariah King 1326263
Hopkins, Byrd Willis 1751121
Hopkins, Katherine Rosborough 17511211
Hopkins, William Rosborough 17511212
Houston, Ashley Holladay 24244523222
Houston, Dorothy ("Dolly") Cromwell Fielden
   242445232
Houston, Dorothy Holladay ("Holly")
   2424452321
Houston, Edward ("Ned") Randolph 2424452323
Houston, Emily Tryon Hoge Booth 242445221
Houston, George Harrison 24244523
Houston, George Harrison, Jr. 242445221
Houston, George Harrison ("Harry"), Jr.
   242445232
Houston, George Harrison ("Harrison") III
   2424452322
Houston, Lynn Luise Ely 2424452322
Houston, Mary Stuart ("Stuey") 242445233
Houston, Mary Stuart Hoge 24244523
Houston, Noel Luise 24244523221
Houston, Parrish Cummings Dobson 242445231
Houston, Peyton Hoge 242445231
Houston, Priscilla Stewart Moore 242445231
Houston, Serin Day 24244523232
Houston, Seth Farwell 24244523231
Houston, Susan Day Farwell 2424452323
Hull, Cary Meriwether Schuler 2424452513
Hull, Charles Lewis 2424452513
Hull, David Sanders 24244525132
Hull, Katherine Schuler 24244525131
Hurst, Janet Elsie 24142x11325

-J-

Jackson, Archie Byron 1326265
Jackson, Archie Byron, Jr. 13262652
Jackson, Barbara Ruth 132626511
Jackson, Davis King 13262651
Jackson, Heather Diane 132626521
Jackson, Helene Kay (Kamama Tsigili)
   132626522

Jackson, Jane 1322133
Jackson, Myrtle Steward 13262651
Jackson, Ruth Scarritt King 1326265
Jackson, Stella Lucille 13262653
Jackson, Willa Helene Kemper 13262652
Jacobs, Ethel Pauline 564211
James, Amanda Rene 24142x113221
James, Anthony O'Dell 24142x11322
James, Anthony O'Dell, Jr. 24142x113223
James, David Alexander 242445262
James, Marilyn Rene Burgess 24142x11322
James, Mary Randolph Mead 242445262
James, Suzzane Joyce 24142x113222
Jarvis, Joan Gay 564211121
Jayne, Jennifer 511182441
Jersak, Gay Clark Anepohl 564211122
Jersak, Paul Eric 564211122
Jiggetts, Susanna Riddick 64111
Johnson, Andrea Elice Beasley 511182421
Johnson, Mark 511182421
Johnston, Elizabeth ("Betsy") Kent McElwain
        2424452521
Johnston, George Randolph Kent 24244525212
Johnston, Laura Tucker Powell 24244525213
Johnston, Oliver Perry Alford 24244525211
Johnston, Randolph Powell 2424452521
Jones, Elizabeth Smithson 36614
Jones, Elmore 36614

-K-

Kean, Betty Faye Miller 24142x173
Kean, Brittney Nicole 24142x1731
Kean, John Michael 24142x173
Kean, Mary Evalina Sanfrosa Prescott
        24142x15
Kearns, Kathleen 242453b115
Kemper, Willa Helene 13262652
Kempker, John Francis Byron 13262652221
Kempker, Laurel Helene Yeager 1326265222
Kempker, Virgil 1326265222
Kettler, Leigh Anne 24244523211
Key, Edith Maxine 51118342
Key, Gerald Wayne 51118341
Key, James 5111836
Key, Jess 5111834
Key, Laura Ann 51118363
Key, Linda 51118361
Key, Melba 51118362
Key, Opal Gladys Williams 5111836
Key, Ruthie Mae Williams 5111834
Keys, Jessie Lee 13444b33
King, Addison Thompson 1326264
King, Addison Thompson, Jr. 13262641
King, Ellen Abell 1326262
King, John 13262643
King, Rev. Joseph 132626
King, Joseph 13262642
King, Mary Catherine 13262644
King, Mary Mariah 1326263
King, Pocahontas Rebecca Cabbell Abell
        White 132626
King, Ruth Cabell 13262645
King, Ruth Mumpower 1326264
KIng, Ruth Scarritt 1326265
Kish, Glenn Paul 6411131114
Kish, Lucy Carmichael Saunders 6411131114

Klattenhoff, Joe George 51118222
Klattenhoff, Kimberly Carol 511182221
Klattenhoff, Linda Janell Hill 51118222
Knauert, David Cromwell 24244523211
Knauert, Dorothy Holladay ("Holly") Houston
        2424452321
Knauert, Fredrick Kurt 2424452321
Knauert, Leigh Anne Kettler 24244523211
Knauert, Melissa Pauline 24244523212
Knauert, Peter Fredrick 242445232111
Knight, Abel McAllister 2122142132
Knight, Beverley Randolph 21221421
Knight, Emily Rachel Dehn 212214212
Knight, Gabrille Dehn 212214212
Knight, Grace Spenser Wells 212214213
Knight, Mary Sommers 212214211
Knight, Maxmilian Gabriel Dehn 2122142121
Knight, Randolph Robbins 212214213
Knight, Samuel Sturdivant 212214213
Knight, William Wilder, Jr. 212214212
Knight, William Wilder Westbury 21221421
Kousis, James Randolph 1344493112
Kousis, Katherine 1344493113
Kousis, Kristine 1344493111
Kousis, Mary Ellen Payne 134449311
Kousis, Nichole Allison 1344493114
Kousis, Peter 134449311
Kramer, Katherine Randolph Stevenson
        2424452123
Kramer, Larry 2424452123
Kramer, Maxwell Bearish 242445211231
Kuda, Daryl 1326265221
Kuda, Darylyn Pristine 13262652211
Kuda, Elizabeth Kay 1326265221

-L-

Lancaster, Ada Carol Littlefield
        24142x1133
Lancaster, Ada Chantel 24142x11331
Lancaster, Gail Patricia Mahaney
        24142x1133
Lancaster, Jane Kean Randolph Butler
        24142x113
Lancaster, Joseph Antonio 24142x11332
Lancaster, Susan Jane 24142x1132
Lancaster, Wesley Cary 24142x1131
Lancaster, Wesley Cleo 24142x113
Lancaster, William Joseph 24142x1133
Layton, Nova 511184
Leedy, Frances Maxine Cobb 13442112
Leedy, Kenneth Marvin 13442112
Leedy, Kenneth Michael 134421122
Leedy, Patricia Ann 134421121
Leonard, Martha 36616
Lewis, Margaret Hunter 24215431
Littlefield, Ada Carol 24142x1133
Long, James Wendell 1322133421
Long, Kate Breckenridge Sampson 1322133421
Lord, John Craik 2424452211
Lord, Julia Mengel Booth Cooke 2424452211
Lujan, Alex 511182412
Lujan, Juvan 5111824121
Lujan, Tanya Elaine Zapata 511182412
Lund, Elizabeth Ashley Schuler Rooney
        2424452511
Lund, Peter 2424452511

36

-M-

Mahaney, Gail Patricia 24142x1133
Mahon, Ethel Pauline Jacobs 564211
Mahon, Ethel Walker 564212
Mahon, Gertrude Agnes 5642113
Mahon, John Adolphus 564211
Mahon, John Adolphus, Jr. 564213
Mahon, Marie Clayton 5642111
Mahon, Susie 5642112
Mann, Frances Cobb 1344212
Mann, Leslie 1344212
Mann, Lois 13442121
Marchese, Emidio 24244521
Marchese, Mary ("Mary San") Randolph 242445211
Marchese, Virginia Randolph Bolling Hoge 24244521
Markham, Frank Devereaux 33152
Markham, Frank Devereaux, Jr. 331522
Marlette, Ethel Pauline 56431112
Marlette, George Clark 5642111
Marlette, Marie Clayton Mahon 5642111
Marlette, Sarah Janice 56421111
Martinisi-Moglia, Virginia 2421545113
Masciocchi, Julian Anthony 64411311221
Masciocchi, Mary Spottswood McClatchey 6411131122
Masciocchi, Stephen Girard 6411131122
Matossian, Cyntia 6411131112
Maxwell, Blane 134421211
Maxwell, Lois Mann Brown 13442121
Maxwell, Robert 13442121
Maxwell, Ryan 134421212
McAllister, Jean Graham 2122142
McBee, Luena 5111831
McCandlish, Frances Archer 25163113
McClain, Andrew J. 51119
McClain, Fortince 511191
McClain, Simen A. Eldridge 51119
McClatchey, John Francis 641113112
McClatchey, Mary Spottswood 6411131122
McClatchey, Susie Baskerville Saunders 641113112
McCulloch (Child) 1344473
McCulloch, Dovie Taylor 1344472
McCulloch, Florence ("Bessie") 13444722
McCulloch, Florence Eveline Bolling 134447
McCulloch, James Wyatt 134447
McCulloch, Lenaeus Bolling 1344471
McCulloch, Mary _____ 13444721
McCulloch, R. H. 1344472
McCulloch, Raymond Bolling 13444721
McElwain, Elizabeth ("Betsy") Kent 2424452521
McElwain, Mary ("Maizy") Randolph Meriwether 242445252
McElwain, Robert Parker 242445252
McIntyre, Mimi Polk Sampson 1322133422
McIntyre, Robert Alan 1322133422
McMahon, Barbara Ann Cobb 13442114
McMahon, Daniel 13442114
McMillian, Marie Corley 511182211
Mead, Anoushka Odette 2424452657
Mead, Barbara Hoge 2424452614
Mead, Carol Ann Vieth 242445264
Mead, Carole K. Rossley 242445261
Mead, Caroline Jackson 2424452633

Mead, Cary Evelyn Hoge 24244526
Mead, Cary Wathen 2424452613
Mead, Charles Cary 242445264
Mead, Charles ("Chip") Jackson 2424452611
Mead, Edith ("Edie") Farwell 2424452651
Mead, Elizabeth ("Betsy") Ellen 2424452642
Mead, Elizabeth ("Sabine") Harmon 24244526!
Mead, George Jackson 24244526
Mead, George Jackson ("Jack II") 242445263
Mead, George Nathaniel Jackson ("Jack") 242445261
Mead, Jacob Farwell ("Cedar") 24244526511
Mead, Jan ("Jay") Willem 2424452651
Mead, Jeremy ("Jerry") Stewart 2424462641
Mead, Johanna ("Hansy") Henrietta Jacoba Van Andel 242445265
Mead, Jonathan Rossley 2424452615
Mead, Joshua ("Josh") Onni Franciscus 2424452658
Mead, Katherine Billingsley Wathen 242445261
Mead, Katherine Elizabeth Craig 2424452653
Mead, Marjorie ("Mimi") Gunn Patterson 242445263
Mead, Mark Nathaniel 2424452652
Mead, Mary Novicki 2424452611
Mead, Mary Randolph 242445262
Mead, Merrill Fowler 2424452632
Mead, Miranda Chefna Carolyn 24244526431
Mead, Morgan Noyes 2424452631
Mead, Peyton Hoge 242445263
Mead, Roanna Margot 2424452656
Mead, Robert ("Bob") Andrew 2424452643
Mead, Samuel ("Sam") Aldo 2424452653
Mead, Sarah ("Sally") Clark Noyes 242445263
Mead, Silas Jan Farwell 2424452612
Mead, Sonya Henrietta 2424452654
Mead, Tanya Georgine 2424452655
Mead, Tracy Thompson 2424452643
Mead, Tristan William Wade 24244526521
Mead, Virginia ("Ginger") Randolph 2424452612
Mead, William Randolph Lacy 242445265
Mead-Fox, Alexander 24244526321
Mead-Fox, Nicholas Payton 24244526322
Mengel, Emily Tryon 24244522
Meriwether, Alexander Williams 24244523311
Meriwether, Cary Mead 2424452334
Meriwether, Edmond Taylor 24244525
Meriwether, Elizabeth Addison Hoge 2424452!
Meriwether, Elizabeth Ellen 24244523341
Meriwether, Elizabeth Hoge 242445251
Meriwether, Erica Tanasijczuk 2424452331
Meriwether, George Houston 2424452333
Meriwether, John Williams 242445233
Meriwether, John Williams, Jr. 2424452331
Meriwether, Kathy Weddell 2424452334
Meriwether, Laura Stuart 24244523342
Meriwether, Mary ("Maizy") Randolph 242445252
Meriwether, Mary Stuart 24244523343
Meriwether, Mary ("Mimi") Stuart 2424452332
Meriwether, Mary Stuart ("Stuey") Houston 242445233
Middleton, Christa Ann Wells 2421545211
Middleton, Connor Ryan 24215452111
Middleton, Frederick McOwen, Jr. 242154521

40

Whitley, Mildred Zachry 13221334
Wiggins, Mary Randolph Emerson 24244521111
Wiggins, Mary Stuart ("Story") 242445211111
Wiggins, Robert 24244521111
Williams, Barbara Elaine 51118371
Williams, Blanch Wasivich 5111837
Williams, Callie 13444a
Williams, Carolyn Sue 51118373
William, Ellen Abell King 1326262
Williams, Estol Wayne 5111838
Williams, Eugene 1326262
Williams, Herbert Howard 5111832
Williams, John Isaac 511183
Williams, Joseph Edward 13262621
Williams, Lester Erskin 5111837
Williams, Luena McBee 5111831
Williams, Lula Smitty 5111833
Williams, Maggie Sue Hill 511183
Williams, Opal Gladys 5111836
Williams, Oscar Raymond 5111831
Williams, Raymond 51118374
Williams, Robert A. 51118372
Williams, Ruby Clare 5111835
Williams, Ruthie Mae 5111834
William, Shirley Skeel 13262621
Williams, Walter Lee 5111833
Wilson, David Randolph 251631134
Wilson, Kelly Robyn 2516311342
Wilson, Ross Patrick 2516311341
Wilson, Susan Holt Strand 251631134
Winston, Caroline ("Carrie") Scott Gay
                                       552312
Winston, Cary Gay 5523123
Winston, Charles Pankey 552312
Winston, Joseph Pendleton 55231
Winston, Mary A. 5523121
Winston, Richard P 5523128
Winston, Virginia Bell 5523124
Winston, Virginia Bell Pankey 55231
Wishon, Jane Mathis Hassell 111326542
Wishon, Keith Steven Wishon 111326542
Wishon, Michael John 1113265423
Wishon, Stephen Donald 1113265422

Womack, Charles 51118351
Womack, Louise Cole 51118351
Woodson, Fannie Greenwood 222312
Wright, Susan Ranae 511182212
Wymore, Montiana Adar Wymore 5111824111
Wymore, Nadia Raylena 5111824112
Wymore, Randy 5111824113
Wymore, Randy Stephen 511182411
Wymore, Rigel Tennyia 5111824115
Wymore, Roxana Lynn Zapata 511182411
Wymore, William Willington 5111824114

-Y-

Yarbrough, Gay Clark Anepohl Jersak
                                    564211122
Yarbrough, Sarah Ann 5642111221
Yarbrough, William Max 564211122
Yeager, Charles Jackson 1326265224
Yeager, Elizabeth Kay 1326265221
Yeager, Helene Kay Jackson 132626522
Yeager, John Edward 132626522
Yeager, John Edward, Jr. 1326265223
Yeager, Laurel Helene 1326265222
Yeager, Morgan Hull 1326265225
Yeager, Nikita Marie 1326265251
Yeager, Stephanie Bosworth 1326265225
Yensen, Amanda Katherine Hall 134449331
Yensen, Doug 134449331
Yensen, Jennifer Hollins 1344493313
Yensen, Johnathan Conrad 1344493312
Yensen, Laura Anne 1344493311

-Z-

Zacharias, Frangis D. 13444b4
Zacharias, Franel Edre 13444b42
Zacharias, Nell Bolling Findley 13444b4
Zapata, Gerald Ochoa 51118241
Zapata, Martha Ann Beasley 51118241
Zapata, Roxana Lynn 511182411
Zapata, Sheryl Denise 511182413
Zapata, Tanya Elaine 511182412
Zigler, Jamie 511182432

SILVER STREAM COUNCIL NO. 18

DEGREE of POCAHONTAS

Imp'd O.R.M.

HUNTING GROUNDS OF
NORFOLK, VA.

13th _Sun_ _Corn_ _Moon_, G.S.D.449.
Common Era _Sept. 13,_ _19 40._

*P*ocahontas' *D*escendants

A Revision, Enlargement and Extension
of the List as Set Out by
Wyndham Robertson in His Book
Pocahontas and Her Descendants (1887)

By Stuart E. Brown, Jr.,
Lorraine F. Myers

FIFTH

Corrections
and
Additions

CLEARFIELD

ACKNOWLEDGEMENTS

Much of the data included in this volume was obtained from or through the assistance of the following persons: John Allen Bolling, Patricia Davies, Gerald Doggett, Anne Hobson Freeman, Frederick Hof, Doris Dee Daugherty Hoge, George Harrison Houston, Jr., Hillyer G. Norment, Lyn L. Swallen, William H. Talley III and Cynthia Walker Wells.

Introduction

The Pocahontas Foundation, based upon information furnished to it, has compiled a tentative list of the descendants of Pocahontas, a list set forth in a combined volume (printed in 1994 and reissued in 1997) which includes reprints of the three books POCAHONTAS' DESCENDANTS (1985), CORRECTIONS AND ADDITIONS TO POCAHONTAS' DESCENDANTS (1992) and SECOND CORRECTIONS AND ADDITIONS TO POCAHONTAS' DESCENDANTS (1994). There is a separate 1997 book, THIRD CORRECTIONS AND ADDITIONS TO POCAHONTAS' DESCENDANTS and a separate 2001 book, FOURTH CORRECTIONS AND ADDITIONS TO POCAHONTAS' DESCENDANTS. The list continues with this FIFTH CORRECTIONS AND ADDITIONS TO POCAHONTAS' DESCENDANTS.

Proposed corrections and/or additions to the list are cordially invited, and should be sent by mail (together with a stamped and addressed envelope) to The Pocahontas Foundation, P. O. Box 431, Berryville, VA 22611.

The Pocahontas Errors
(noted in FOURTH CORRECTIONS AND ADDITIONS)

There is in the Virginia Historical Society an Elmo Jones black and white drawing showing Pocahontas being traded for a copper kettle and depicting her, probably erroneously, as dressed rather fully clothed and in moccasins.

Thomas Bolling of "Cobbs" (1735-1804) (11)

Courtesy: Colonial Williamsburg Foundation

Elizabeth ("Betty") Gay Bolling (1738-1813) (42)
(Mrs. Thomas Bolling) with twins Sarah (118) and Ann (119)

Courtesy: Colonial Williamsburg Foundation

FIFTH CORRECTIONS AND ADDITIONS TO POCAHONTAS' DESCENDANTS
and/or CORRECTIONS AND ADDITIONS and/or
SECOND CORRECTIONS AND ADDITIONS and/or
THIRD CORRECTIONS AND ADDITIONS and/or
FOURTH CORRECTIONS AND ADDITIONS

1321   Sophonisba E. Cabell, m. Robert Harrison Hanson Grayson
(3/12/1780-1826)

13211 William Powhatan Bolling Grayson (b. Little Sandy Salt
Works, Greenup County, KY-1872), m. Susan Dixon (ca. 1816-
6/20/1891), dau. of Capt. Henry and Mary Johnston Dixon of
Henderson County. Home: Henderson County. He was a
Confederate Colonel who was captured and put on a
$20,000.00 bond, but in 1865, he was rearrested for an
alleged violation of his bond, and sued for his bond. His
Fernwood Cemetery gravestone shows Powhattan.

132112 Mary Eleanor Grayson (b. probably in Henderson County-
d. 3/6/1906), m. her first cousin, Capt. ("Captain Hal")
Henry Dixon (ca. 1836, in KY-4/21/1904 in Henderson
County), son of John Robert and Sarah Elizabeth G. Powell
Dixon. Home: Evansville, IN. They had several children.

132114 Susan Bailie Grayson (b. 12/25/1843, in KY-   ), m. William
G. Norment (b. ca. 1829 in Mecklenburg County, VA - d.
between 1881-1900), son of Achilles James and Mary Gunn
Jeffries Norment. He was a farmer. Home: Henderson.

1321141 Lee F. Norment (b. ca. 1865, probably in Henderson County-
d. 6/14/1906, of a railroad accident). Bur. Henderson.

1321142 Phelps Norment (b. 9/ /1867, probably in Henderson County-
), m. ca. 1893, Bobbie_____ (b. 4/ /1876, in
KY-   ). He was a farm laborer.

13211421 Blanch Norment (9/ /1894-   )

13211422 Thomas Norment (12/ /1896-   )

13211423 Phelps Norment, Jr. (5/ /1898-   )

1321143 Achilles J.Norment (ca. 1868-9/18/1878). B. and d. in
Henderson County.

1321144 William G. Norment, Jr. (ca. 12/ /1869, probably in
Henderson County-   )

1321145 Robert Norment (ca. 1871, in KY-   )

1321146 Eliza Norment (ca. 1875, in KY-   )

1321147 Lucy Norment (ca. 1878, in KY-   )

1321148 Annie S. Norment (11/ /1881, probably in Henderson
County-   ), m. 5/9/1900, Charles R. Shanke. Home:
Toledo, OH

132115 Sophonisba ("Sophy") E. Grayson (11/9/1845-4/20/1931) (b.
and d. in Henderson County), m. James Monroe Watson
(1839-3/23/1919) (b. and d. in Henderson County), son of
Dr. William Price and Jane Thomas Watson. He was a
farmer.

1321151 Grayson P. Watson (7/5/1862-3/5/1912). Henderson County.

1321152 Jennie Watson, m. Howell C. Watson (4/19/1856,in AR-
7/14/1943, in Henderson)

1321153   Mary ("Mollie") H. Watson (1/19/1866, in KY-10/20/1938, in
          Henderson), m. Charles Milton Grimes (8/25/1859, in
          Montgomery County, KY-8/18/1927, in Henderson County),
          son of Ben F. and Mary K. Dooley Grimes.
1321154   Bertha Watson (7/4/1870, in KY-6/29/1942, in Henderson
          County), m. John Stanley Dennis (6/26/1864, in KY-6/24/
          1932, in Henderson County). HOme: Henderson County.
1321155   Tony Watson (ca. 1875, in KY-   )
132116   Hebe Carter Grayson (d. 2/27/1905), m. (1st) Colonel
          DeMiller; m. (2nd) William Butler; m. (3rd) Colonel
          Grimes (from AR)
132118   Elizabeth Cabell Grayson (b. ca. 1849-   )

13211a   Roger Dixon Grayson (d. 1/29/1935), m. Mayme Grimes (1/9/
          1865, in MO-3/24/1938 in Henderson County), dau. of Ben F.
          and Mary K. Dooley Grimes.

13213   Hebe Carter Grayson (d. 1871), m. (1st) William Preston
          Smith (1805-1850); m. (2nd) William Peartree Smith (8/19/
          1808-12/12/1861), son of Col. Obadiah Smith

13213133 Edith Ogden Harrison (1/21/1896-   )

132131x   Sophonisba Preston Harrison (b. Heidelberg, Germany)

1321x6   Robert Grayson Adams (d. 11/28/1896), m. Martha ("Mattie")
          Elam

1344   Robert Markham Bolling, m. (3rd) Frances Brackett (1809 or
          1810-1851) of Cumberland County, m. (4th) Francis P.

13442   Susan Peyton Bolling (1851-ca. 1911)
          Child by third wife of 1344
13443   Robert Bolling, Jr. (1945 or 1946-   )

1711   Bolling Starke Dandridge of Hanover County (1812-1876), m.
          (2nd) 4/10/1840, in Goochland County, Elizabeth Ann Bowles
          (-9/20/1908), dau. of Charles Knight and Lucy Price
          Jackson Bowles. Both bur. Teays Hill Cemetery, St. Albans,
          Kanawha County, WV
17111   Laura Dandridge (1841 in Goochland County-   ), m. 6/16/
          1863, in Louisa County, Peter D. Woodson.
17112   Lucy M. Dandridge (1843-   ), m. 1/18/1869, in Richmond,
          Elisha Henry Pendleton (ca. 1832 in Va.-   )
171121   Elizabeth Bolling Pendleton (7/28/1872-12/29/1957), m.
          (1st) 10/26/1898, Clarence Rader. M. (2nd) 3/19/1918,
          William Wood
1711211   Lynn P. Rader (1899-5/18/1963), m. Margaret Ruth _____
17112111 Elizabeth Rader

171122   Charles William Pendleton (5/26/1878-7/10/1970 in Braden-
          ton, FL), m. 6/14/1899, Margaret Kerns (2/20/1878, in VA-
          4/2/1936 in Washington, DC)

1711221 Guy Briggs Pendleton (6/27/1900, in St. Albans-3/20/1949 in Bradenton), m. 9/18/1928, Ava Irene Summers (1/11/1907-5/24/1988, b. and d. in Hagerstown, MD)

17112211 Guy Briggs Pendleton, Jr. (6/19/1929-1/6/1998). Unm.

17112212 Patsy Ann Pendleton (2/22/1931-8/29/1991), m. 7/16/1955, Terrence Walker Rogers

171122121 John Alden Rogers (8/21/1957-   ), m. Leslie _____

1711221211 Amber Rogers

1711221212 Miles Arthur Rogers (7/23/1996-   )

171122122 James Allen Rogers (1/10/1960-   )

17112213 Jack Edward Pendleton (2/23/1933-1/13/1992), m. 2/4/1956, Pearl Louise Kauffman

171122131 Robert Emerson Pendleton (9/11/1959-   ), m. 11/23/1985, Amy Sue Miller

17112214 James Robert Pendleton (2/7/1943, in Hagerstown, MD-   ), m. 7/6/1968, Pamela Sue Killin (12/29/1947, in Niagra Falls-   )

171122141 Stephanie Sue Pendleton (9/11/1973-   ), m. 12/18/1993, Richard Anthony Marquiss (11/30/1973-   )

1711221411 Eden Nicole Marquiss (11/19/1996-   )

1711221412 Logene Elizabeth Marquiss (2/26/1999-   )

1711222 William Vernon Pendleton (11/11/1902-9/14/1955), m. 1/26/1929, Edna Rhae Gossard

17112221 Warren Samuel Pendleton (3/4/1931-11/29/1991), m. Carolyn Ann Fifer

171122211 Debra Carole Pendleton, m. _____ Wade

171122212 Warren Samuel Pendleton, Jr.

171122213 Dorothy Anne Pendleton

171122214 Glenda Fay Pendleton, m. _____ Sherman

171122215 Brenda Jeanne Pendleton,m. _____ Turner

17112222 William Vernon Pendleton, Jr. (1/23/1936-5/19/1983). Unm.

17113 Julia C. Dandridge (1846-   )

17114 Bettie Bolling Dandridge (3/9/1850-10/3/1942). Unm. Bur. St. Albans

17115 Thomasia L. Dandridge (1851-   )

17116 Charles S. Dandridge (1855-   )

17117 Sarah ("Sallie") Dandridge (3/16/1859, in Goochland County-3/21/1942) (bur. St. Albans), m. 2/24/1888, Murray Briggs

21936 Thomas Bolling, Jr., m. 5/27/1878, Sallie Bennett Aylett, dau. of Patrick Henry and Emily Ann Coles Rutherfoord Aylett

219361 Randolph Bolling (d.7/10/1937), bur. Hollywood Cemetery, m. (1st) Sally B. Stokes, m. (2nd) Suzie Annie Estelle Peppett (9/25/1876-12/31/1933), dau. of Joseph Weaver and Annie Forman Elmira Moore Peppett

2193611 Estelle Randolph Bolling (b. in Canada-d. 3/ /1969, in New Hampshire), m. (1st) Dr. Willard E. Austen, m. (2nd) Henry Longfellow DeRham

2193612 Thomas B. Bolling (b. in Canada, d. 10/ /1972, in France), m. Janet Adair Nicholson (9/22/1919-11/13/1964). Ashes scattered on graves of wife and children.

21936121 Thomas Randolph Bolling (10/4/1952-11/13/1964)

21936122 Ellen Nicholson Bolling (8/8/1955-11/13/1964). Janet Adair Nicholson and her two children, Thomas Randolph and Ellen Nicholson, all died as the result of a fire at their home in Pluckemin, Nr. Peapack, NJ, when Thomas B. Bolling was away at sea.

2193613 Josephine Peppett Bolling (b. in Canada, d. 4/5/1986, in England), m. 9/25/1928, Lt. Commander Hugh M. Davies

21936131 Hugh Walter Davies (7/17/1929-   ), b. in Nova Scotia, m. 1953, Patricia Helen Kease (9/10/1032-   ), of Devon, England

219361311 Hugh Jonathan Edward Davies (5/14/1954-   ), of Hampshire, England, m. 1977, Coral Synnott (3/23/1955-   ), of England

219361312 Mark Timothy Davies (12/15/1956-   ), of Dorset, England

2424452 Rev. Peyton Harrison Hoge (d. 10/12/1940)

24244521 Virginia Randolph Bolling Hoge, m. the machese Emidio San Germano in Arpino, Italy

242445211 Mary ("Mary San") Randolph San Germano, m. Warwick McNair Anderson

2424452111 Mary Stuart ("Stuey") Anderson, m. George Waldo Emerson (d. 5/7/2002)

24244522232 Stuart Selden Walker, m. 12/12/2000, Tracey Ann Foulger (4/10/1972-   )

24244523 Mary Stuart ("Honey") Hoge

242445232112 George Harrison Knavert (8/25/2000-   )

242445232113 Lillian Ward Knavert (8/25/2000-   )

2424452411 Peyton Harrison Hoge IV. Div. (around 1962) Mary Ellen Breen

24244524112 Peyton Harrison Hoge V, m. 6/10/2000, Jennifer Ruth Karem

2424452513 Elizabeth ("Libba") Knight Hoge (1950-   )

2424452414 Blanche Smith Hoge, m. 12/27/1976, Joseph Hamilton
Pedigo III

24244524152 Virginia Buchanan Gerhart, m. 9/22/2001, Daniel W.
Statham

24245525 Elizabeth Addison ("Bessie") Hoge

242445251211 Hanna Elizabeth Burnett (9/9/2000-   ) (twin)
242445251212 Lily Christine Burnett (9/9/2000-   ) (twin)

2424452611 Charles ("Chip") Jackson Mead, m. Mary Navickis
24244526111 Ashley Navickis Mead (9/26/1999-   )

24244526125 Donald Benjamin Cary Schmitt (6/3/1984-   )
24244526126 Mathew Oliver Schmitt (12/8/1985-   )
24244526127 Johannal Elizabeth Schmitt (10/15/1997-   )
24244526128 Jeremiah Nathaniel Schmitt (11/28/1997-   )
24244526129 Joshau Paul Schmitt (10/23/1998-   )
NOTE: The names may be Schmidt.

24244526131 Caitlee FengYi Mead (10/29/1995-   )
24244526132 Ceaghan DieuLinh Mead (11/19/1997-   )

2424452614 Barbara Hoge Mead, m. 3/21/1998, Jean-Francois Paris
(10/8/1951-   )

24244526331 Laura Caroline Gunnels
24244526332 Jennifer Clarke Gunnels
24244526333 Brandon Marc Gunnels
2424452642 Elizabeth ("Betsy") Ellen Mead, m. Armando Maldonado

24244526521 Isabel Margot Mead (1/29/2001-   )

24244526531 Ruby Eliza Mead (7/19/2001-   )

2424452655 Tanya Georgine Mead, m. 10/20/2001, Braulio Garcia
(3/26/1962-   )

323   Susanna ("Sukey") Fleming, m. Capt. Addison Lewis who died on
       9/26/1781. He was killed the month before Yorktown.
3231   Susan Lewis, m. William Powel Byrd (d. 1815)

3231211 Richard Coke Marshall was not a Colonel, C.S.A. In later
         life he became an honorary Captain of the Portsmouth Fire
         Department. M. 11/21/1865, Mary Catherine Wilson.

323121142   Mary Douthat Marshall (d. 4/27/1996), m. 8/24/1926,
            Joseph Reid Anderson Hobson, Jr. (9/14/1901-10/30/
            1986), son of Joseph Reid Anderson and Annie Lee
            Camm Hobson of Richmond.
323121142a Mary Marshall Hobson (1929-1929)
3231211421 Susan Lewis Hobson (d. 3/11/2002), m. 7/31/1954, Colin
            Wallace McCord (5/15/1928-   )
32312114211 Mary Marshall McCord (9/22/1956-   ), m. 5/24/1986,
            Alexander Lewis Okun (6/17/1957-   )
323121142111 Ada Elizabeth Okun (1/6/1989-   )
323121142112 Evan Andrew Okun (7/30/1991-   )
32312114212 Andrew King McCord (1/5/1958-   ), m. 7/10/1993,
            Emily Singer (7/2/1957-   )
323121142121 Rebecca Maya McCord (6/5/1995-   )
323121142122 Elizabeth Anne McCord (1/4/1999-   )
32312114213 Anne Camm McCord (7/1/1965-   ), due to marry on
            6/21/2003, Ray Rue
3231211422 Anne Colston Hobson (3/19/1934-   ), m. 12/6/1958,
            George Clemon Freeman, Jr. (1/3/1929-   ), son of
            George Clemon and Annie Laurie Gill Freeman of
            Birmingham
32312114221 Anne Colston Freeman (10/2/1960-   ), m. 5/23/1987,
            Colin McEvoy (6/24/1961-   ), son of George and
            Patricia Bernard McEvoy of Duxbury, MA
323121142211 George Connor McEvoy (11-22-1991-   )
323121142212 Anne Colston McEvoy (6/27/1995-   )
323121142213 John Marshall McEvoy (9/25/1997-   )
323121142214 Mark Andrew McEvoy (3/7/2000-   )
32312114222 George Clemon Freeman III (5/28/1963-   ), m. 5/19/
            1990, Louise Gilbert (2/6/1983-   ), dau. of John
            and Harriet Sloop Gilbert of Statesville, NC
323121142221 Sara Pressly Freeman (7/2/1991-   )
323121142222 Katherine Colston Freeman (3/31/1993-   )
323121142223 George Clemon Freeman IV (2/22/2002-   )
32312114223 Joseph Reid Anderson Freeman (10/15/1965-   ), due to
            marry on 10/4/2003, Alexandra Anton Barker (4/12/
            1971-   )

36631 Sarah Ann Morris, m. 8/11/1842, Isaac Bennett. As recorded
       in Highland County, Ohio, and written about by Ella M.
       Doggett Hostetler in her family history books. Ella was
       a contemporary of Mr. and Mrs. William Morris and their
       daughter and son-in-law, Sarah and Isaac Bennett. Isaac
       lived about one mile west of Hillsboro on the Cincinnatti
       Pike.   William would walk to Isaac's home and they would
       walk together into town. It gave their horses a rest on

the day they went into town. Both the William Morris' and the Isaac Bennetts lived in HIghland County when she was a child. They were her step great grand and step grandparents. Her own mother passed away in April, 1866, and her father remarried the following September 1, 1866, the oldest daughter of Isaac and Sarah Ann Bennett, Sarah Jane Bennett. In the barn yard of the Morris' sat several Conestoga wagons . . . very well and heavily built . . . full of rusting iron . . . they were used by the Morris' and the other people who emigrated with them from the eastern peninsula of Maryland sometime after the end of the Revolutionary War to settle in Ohio. Sarah Jane Bennett Doggett became Ella and her brother, Charlie's step mother. I have seen the graves of both Charlie, who died as a teenager, and his mother, Mary Ellen Huffman Doggett, in the graveyard in Hillsboro. We visited the farm site where Cary and Sarah Jane Doggett lived east of Hillsboro.

366311   Sarah Jane Bennett (5/17/1843-12/7/1896), m. 9/1/1866, Cary Armstead Doggett (4/23/1823=6/22/1887)

3663111   Isaac ("Ike") Bennett Daggett (6/28/1867-9/5/1953), m. 11/9/1891, Ida Mahalia Marks (NOTE: Isaac changed his name from DOGGETT to DAGGETT).

36631111   Opal Daggett (d. 1918), m. August Schuman (d. 1970's)

366311111   Velma Schuman (10/31/1917-11/9/2001), m. Harlan H. Hansen

3663111111   Carol Hansen (1/12/1944-   )

3663111112   Robert ("Bob") Hansen (9/26/1946-   ), m. Carol Nelson (11/10/1948 or 1949-   )

36631111121   Marnie Shawn Hansen (12/30/1967-   )

36631112   Edith Daggett (3/7/1896-   ), m. 2/20/1929, Fred Schuman (6/26/1896-   )

366311121   Dorothy Elaine Schuman (7/27/1931-   ), m. 7/ /1949, Rodney Gallagher

3663111211   Candice R. Gallagher (12/25/1950-   ), m. (1st) Gerald Madden. M. (2nd) David Fanning

36631112111   Shelley Madden (7/41971-   ), m. 11/1/1997, Brett Figueroa

366311121111   Garrett Nel Figueroa (9/21/1998-   )

366311121112   Grant Corbett Figueroa (5/8/2001-   )

36631112112   Amy Madden (5/1/1976-   ), m. Troy Shaklee

366311122   Donald Fred Schuman (5/30/1939-   ), m. Sandra Rose

36631113   Ella Mae Daggett (3/7/1896-5/11/1989), m. 1/1/1921, Carl Lloyd Witt (4/22/1898-7/19/1978)

366311131   Willa June Witt (6/1/1923-6/12/1995), m. 4/27/1947, Clarence Loy Stancil (10131910-3/11/1993)

3663111311   Albert Wesley Stancil (9/22/1948-   ), m. (1st) 6/ / 1967, Terie Sue Mattingly (10/17/1950-   ). M. (2nd) 8/21/1971, Nancy Ann MacDonald (8/12/1949-   )

36631113111   Melissa Sue Stancil (11/13/1967-   ), m. 10/6/1996, John Northscott Street III (11/4/1965-   )

366311131111   Amanda Nicole Street (11/14/1995-   )

36631113112   Aileen Johanna Stancil (5/5/1973-   ), m. 7/2/1995, Dean Patrick Wrench (3/28/1971-   )

3663111312 Susan June Stancil (3/22/1950-   ), m. (1st) 12/16/
            1967, George Darcy Paoletti (10/24/1948-   ). M.
            (2nd) 10/29/1971, Robert Monaco II (3/22/1945-6/ /
            1993). M. (3rd) 1/20/2001, Thomas Francis McCloskey
36631113121 Steven Dylan Paoletti (11/29/1968-   ), m. 10/1/
            1994, Heidi Elise Wolfe (2/4/1968-   )
366311131211 Lily Hope Paoletti (11/7/1999-   )
366311131212 Child (b. 8/26/2001-   )
3663111313 Richard Dean Stancil (1117/1954-   ), m. 1/16/1976,
            Gina Susan Bertrand (12/14/1957-   )
36631113131 Joshua Richard Stancil (7/1/1976-   ), m. (1st) 5/ /
            1995, Ellen _____. M. (2nd) Cinnamon Myers (3/1/
            1973-   )
366311131311 Justin Tyler Stancil (8/29/1995-   )
366311131312 Rebecca Ann Stancil (8/29/2000-   )
36631113132 Jesse Clayton Stancil (2/3/1978-   )
36631113133 Adam Cody Stancil (2/15/1982-   ), m. 11/17/2000,
            Chantal Post (3/5/1982-   )
366311131331 Angelyna Dae Stancil (8/17/2002-   )
366311132 Marvin Carl Witt (5/8/1924-   ), m. 9/ /1947, Doris
            Ellen Weaver (9/6/1927-   )
3663111321 Doris Elizabeth Witt (7/27/1955-   ), m. 4/15/1978,
            Michael John Sullivan (7/19/1944-   )
3663111322 Brian Carl Witt (11/2/1957-   )
36631114   Warren LeRoy Daggett (3/1/1900-8/1/1982)
3663112   Mary Elizabeth Doggett (12/15/1868-12/2/1952), m. 6/18/
            1889, Lincoln Marsden (1866-1929)
36631121   Virgie L. Marsden (1890-1981), m. Clyde Mead (1885-1967)
366311211 Kenneth Mead (1910-   ), m. Adeline _____ (1903-
            1961)
3663112111 Wanda Mead
3663112112 Marsda Mead
366311212 Clyde Mead, Jr. (1914-   ), m. Mary _____(deceased)
3663112121 Mary Kay Mead
36631122   Earl Marsden (1892-   ), m. Mary _____(deceased)
366311221 Max Marsden (1916-deceased), m. Mary _____(deceased)
3663112211 Patricia Marsden
3663112212 Marcia Marsden
36631123   Georgia L. Marsden (1894-1978), m. Charles Bowlyow (1882-
            1977)
366311231 C. Earl Bowlyow (1915-2002), m. Helen Eaves (1921-   )
3663112311 Cary L. Bowlyow
3663112312 Charles L. Bowlyow
3663112313 Richard E. Bowlyow
3663112314 Jerry L. Bowlyow
3663112315 Byron O. Bowlyow
366311232 Gail F. Bowlyow (1917-1980), m. Betty L. Glendening
            1925-1980)
3663112321 Ronald G. Bowlyow (1943-   ), m. Jane _____(1947-   )
36631123211 Kent Bowlyow (1968-1980)
            Chad Bowlyow (1973-   ) (Adopted)
3663112322 Bonnie S. Bowlyow (1944-   ), m. Loren Johnson (1944-
). Div.
36631123221 Angela Johnson (1964-   ), m. David Alberts (1963-   )

```
366311232211  Justin Alberts (1997-      )
36631123222   Amy Johnson (1966-      ), m. Michael Schmitz (1957-    )
3663112323    Joyce E. Beaulieu (Changed name back to original
              French) (1952-      )
3663112324    Peggy A. Bowlyow (1954-      ), m. Donald Ingles (1950-
              )
36631123241   Gretchen Ingles (1974-      ), m. Paul Peterson (1970-
              )
366311232411  Kristen Peterson (1994-      )
366311232412  Eric Peterson (1997-      )
366311232413  Mariah Peterson (2002-      )
36631123242   Sarah Ingles (1978-      ), m. Kory Nichols (1978-      )
366311232421  Noah Nichols (2001-      )
3663112325    Jill R. Bowlyow (1957-      ), m. (1st) Randy Ingles
              1958-      ). M. (2nd) John Lenahan (1955-      )
36631123251   Jennifer Ingles (1980-      )
36631123252   Michael Lenahan (1984-      )
36631123253   Christopher Lenahan (1984-      )
366311233     Mary L. Bowlyow (1918-      ), m. John F. Clover II (1909-
              1968)
3663112331    John F. Clover III (1941-      ), m. (1st) Betty _____.
              Div. M. (2nd) Cheryl
36631123311   Tammy Clover
36631123312   John F. Clover IV
36631123313   Jason Clover
366311234     Doris Bowlyow (1924-      ), m. Raymond West (1924-      )
3663112341    Judy West (1950-      )
3663112342    Mike West (1953-      )
36631124      Frank Marsden (1900-1986), m. G. Mona Dixon (1898-1984)
366311241     Jacqueline Marsden (1922-1936)
366311242     Jean Marsden (1925-      ), m. Richard Stone (1924-2001)
3663113       Maggie Marie Doggett (8/10/1871-9/27/1966), m. (1st) 7/3/
              1889, James John Smeltzer (     -2/4/1899). M. (2nd)
              12/28/1899, John E. Shellhammer (7/19/1855-10/6/1931)
36631131      Hazel Mildred Smeltzer (4/21/1890-3/ /1779), m. Ralph
              Randall Shellhammer
366311311     Florence Shellhammer
366311312     Elsie Shellhammer
366311313     John Shellhammer
366311314     Fay Shellhammer
366311315     Twila Shellhammer
366311316     Frank Shellhammer
366311317     Roy Shellhammer
366311318     Baby (died)
366311319     Phyllis Shellhammer, m. Mr. Keibler
36631132      Ruth Irene Smeltzer (9/6/1893-1/14/1985), m. Harley
              Boorman
366311321     George Boorman (11/4/1914-4/9/1998), m. Dorothy _____
              (1918-11/27/1993)
3663113211    Judith Boorman, m. 8/ /1989, Bradley Bock
366311322     Ralph Boorman (8/27/1916-10/23/2002), m. 11/30/1939,
              Grace Yeager (7/15/1918-3/7/1991)
3663113221    Gayle Boorman (2/19/1943-      ), m. 9/2/1962, Daniel
              Rogalski (1/ /1938-      )
```

36631132211 Mark Rogalski (12/23/1964-   ), m. 1/ /1996, Beth
                        ‾‾‾‾‾‾‾‾
366311322111 Arron Rogalski
366311322112 Joshua Rogalski
366311322113 Elsie Rogalski
36631132212 David Rogalski (11/10/1969-   ), m. 7/ /2000, Jessica
                Herron
36631132213 Kenneth Rogalski (3/3/1973-   )
3663113222 Barbara Boorman (9/4/1943-   ), m. 9/ /1963, Raymond
                Moonan (1/10/1943-2/1/2003) (Div.)
366311322211 John Robert Moonan (1998-   )
36631132222 Deborah Moonan (1/1/1968-   ), m. (1st) Daryl Starnes.
                Div. M. (2nd) Terry Woodall
366311322221 Joel Starnes (10/1/1989)
366311322222 Erika ‾‾‾‾‾‾‾‾‾‾‾
3663113223 Gary Boorman (4/18/1948-   ), m. 11/26/1970, Gail
                Norton (2/2/1950-   )
36631132231 Andrew Graham Boorman (2/19/1981-   )
36631132232 Jeremy Glendon Boorman (11/3/1983-   ) (twin)
36631132233 Brian Gregory Boorman (11/3/1983-   ) (twin)
366311323 Hazel Boorman, m. (1st) Stanley Rushnov. M. (2nd)
                Richard Roby
3663113231 Candice Rushnov, m. (1st) George ‾‾‾‾‾‾‾‾‾‾. M. (2nd)
                Edward Holloway
36631132311 Richard ‾‾‾‾‾‾‾‾‾‾‾
36631132312 Jennifer Rushnov, m. (1st) ‾‾‾‾‾‾‾‾‾‾‾‾. M. (2nd)
                Droney ‾‾‾‾‾‾‾‾‾‾‾
366311323121 (Child)
366311323122 Nicole ‾‾‾‾‾‾‾‾‾‾‾
366311324 Harley Nick Boorman (9/9/1926-   ), m. Jean Flora
                Schubert (9/14/1928-   )
3663113241 Thomas John Boorman (8/26/1952-   ), m. Sheila Gail
                Chartier (3/14/1956-   )
36631132411 Kristen Nicole Boorman (2/12/1987-   )
                Jennifer Boorman (Adopted)
                Michelle Boorman (Adopted)
3663113242 Peter James Boorman (9/26/1953-   ), m. Ellen Lynn
                Connery (6/19/1954-   )
36631132421 Nicholas Connery Boorman (6/9/1987-   )
36631132422 Zachary Connery Boorman (8/30/1991-   )
3663113243 James Lewis Boorman (1/26/1955-   ), m. Lynn Marie
                Driscoll (3/23/1955-   )
36631132431 Ryan Matthew Boorman (5/13/1982-   )
36631132432 Stephanie Jean Boorman (3/10/1984-   )
3663113244 Frederick ("Freddy") Boorman (9/14/1956-   ), m.
                Deborah Cable (11/13/1956-   )
36631132441 Timothy Boorman (11/23/1983-   )
36631132442 Katherine Boorman (6/22/1986-   )
36631132443 Erika Boorman (2/14/1992-   )
36631132444 Emily Boorman (3/21/1990-   )
3663113245 Brian Michael Boorman (11/30/1958-   ), m. Patricia
                Wronski (8/30/1958-   )

```
36631132451  Joyce Jean Boorman (8/11/1986-    )
36631132452  Elizabeth Jean Boorman (8/2/1988-    )
36631132453  Stephen Nicholas Boorman (11/28/1989-    )
36631132454  Caroline Jean Boorman (1/7/1992-    )
36631133  Esther Jean Smeltzer (12/30/1895-8/18/1979), m. Frank
          Shutt
366311331  Dorothy Shutt, m. Eugene Beatty
3663113311  Donna Shutt, m. _____ Waltenbach
36631133111  Amy Waltenbach
3663113312  Bill Beatty, m._____
36631133121  Billy Beatty, m. Heidi _____
366311331211  Child
366311331212  Child
366311331213  Child
366311332  Dale Shutt (7/4/    -    ), m. _____ Miller
3663113321  Daughter
366311333  Donald Eugene Shutt (8/21/1924-    )
36631134  William Jennings Smeltzer (1/2/1898-6/14/1898)
36631135  Ella Marie Shellhammer (7/13/1906-    ), m. 10/25/1928,
          Fred Wareham (7/9/1902-1/11/2000)
366311351  Oris OraLou Wareham (4/14/1931-    ), m. Roger Pattison
          (Sr.?)
3663113511  Roger Pattison
3663113512  Cynthia Pattison
3663113513  Christine Pattison
366311352  Francis Elfred Wareham (7/25/1934-9/30/1997), m. 9/4/
          1955, Marilyn June Millay (6/17/1935-    )
3663113521  Joan Marie Warham (5/8/1957-    ), m. 8/27/1994, Walt
          Alan Prouix (11/6/1963-    )
36631135211  Austin Prouix (8/12/1996-    )
3663113522  Jeffery March Wareham (1/18/1960-    ), m. 11/10/1983,
          Mariaelena Gonzolez (2/10/1960-    )
36631135221  Shea Wareham (8/11/1983-    )
36631135222  Shaun Wareham (2/17/1985-    )
3663113523  Judy Lynn Wareham (4/14/1961-    ), m. 7/30/1988, Kelly
          Kordel Kight (9/1/1962-    )
36631135231  Chelsea Kight (4/20/1990-    )
36631135232  Kaelyn Kight (12/6/1992-    )
3663113524  Jill Kay Wareham (5/8/1963-    ), m. 5/30/1993, Craig
          Alan Walter (10/2/1964-    )
36631135241  Rylee Walter (11/4/1995-    )
36631135242  Jarret Walter (2/12/1998-    )
366311353  Loretta Wareham, m. Steven Hawley
3663113531  Jimmy Hawley, m.
3663113532  Suzanne Hawley
36631136  Nora Loretta Shellhammer (8/27/1914-    ), m. Donald T.
          Adams (    -1981)
3663114  James Livy Boyd Doggett (9/26/1873-8/19/1946), m. 1/30/
          1901, Alice Margaret Austin (7/10/1882-2/26/1968)
36631141  Harlow Harry Doggett (11/6/1901-3/6/1984), m. (1st) 3/10/
          1923, Osa Mae Garretson (7/27/1901-6/29/1940)
366311411  Max Ray Doggett (1/12/1924-    ), m. 6/14/1953, Harvenna
          ("Bonnie") Whiteman (11/4/1931-    )
```

```
3663114111  Tina Rae Doggett (2/22/1955-    ), m. 10/9/1982, Rodney
            Darrell Kurtzer (11/1/1954-    )
36631141111 Cherry LaRae Kurtzer (5/5/1984-    )
36631141112 Wendy Lee Kurtzer (1/4/1988-    )
36631141113 Will Landon Kurtzer (9/12/1991-    )
3663114112  Joy Dawn Doggett (6/29/1956-    ), m. 1/31/1996, Fred
            Wrightsil (2/5/1946-    )
3663114113  Randy Robin Doggett (9/29/1958-    ), m. 7/21/1978, Ida
            Elaine _____
36631141131 Jesse Joe Doggett (4/12/1980-    )
36631141132 Dusty Lee Doggett (7/4/1981-    )
36631141133 Candice Ann Doggett (9/9/1987-    )
3663114114  Casey Joe Doggett (8/24/1961-    ), m. 2/15/1986, Janet
            Zulkoski
36631141141 Ethan Doggett (10/29/1990-    )
36631141142 Douglas Doggett (4/4/1987-    )
3663114115  Gloria Kay Doggett (6/2/1967-    ), m. 6/1/1985, Marvin
            Lee Olson (9/28/1960-    )
36631141151 Nathan Lee Olson (4/27/1989-    )
36631141152 Katie Mae Olson (9/28/1993-    )
36631141153 Mitchaella Olson (5/13/1997-    )
36631141154 Juanetia Olson ( / /2000-    )
366311412   Gale James Doggett (12/24/1926-    ), m. 2/14/1948, Erma
            Colleen Crosby (10/20/1929-    )
3663114121  Timothy Jay Doggett (8/21/1948-6/21/1962)
3663114122  Terry Allen Doggett (2/22/1953-9/10/1975)
3663114123  Rex Lavern Doggett (12/25/1953-    ), m. (1st) 9/17/
            1972, Cheryl Ann Madson (7/28/1954-    ). M (2nd)
            7/21/1985, Marcia Ann Edwards (4/19/1956-    )
36631141231 Karri Rose Doggett (3/4/1977-11/9/1979)
36631141232 Rawley James Doggett (4/20/1980-    )
36631141233 Casey Ryan Doggett (6/4/1981-    )
36631141234 Timothy Lyle Doggett (10/20/1988-    )
36631141235 Benjamin William Doggett (3/16/1993-    )
3663114124  Jack Bryan Doggett (3/18/1958-    ), m. (1st) 9/6/1980,
            Vicki Joe Anderson (1/21/1957-    ). M. (2nd) 6/1/
            1985, Arminda Lucille Lester (9/16/1959-    )
36631141241 Justin Luke Doggett (10/16/1981-    ) (twin)
36631141242 Jed Caleb Doggett (10/16/1981-    ) (twin)
36631141243 Cody Bryan Doggett (11/11/1985-    )
36631141244 Ryan Clark Doggett (3/12/1987-    )
3663114125  Brett Russell Doggett (b. and d. 5/3/1962)
3663114126  Michael Dale Doggett (11/1/1963-    ), m. (1st) Darla
            Ramstad (4/26/1959-    ). M. (2nd) 4/1/1989, Mary
            Kathryn Logian (4/19/1962-    )
36631141261 Dustin Robert Brauneis (7/5/1980-    )
36631141262 Laken Coleen Doggett (2/10/1992-    )
366311413   Dick Laurence Doggett (2/24/1929-    ), m. 2/7/1948,
            Elaine Alvera Simons (4/13/1928-    )
3663114131  Gerald Laurence Doggett (11/9/1948-    ), m. 12/12/1987,
            Teresa Marie Butts (6/9/1957-    )
3663114132  Beverly Jean Doggett (6/23/1951-    ), m. 2/12/1972,
            Dwight Ray Brown (11/17/1949-    )
```

```
36631141321  Dustin Ray Brown (11/13/1972-    )
36631141322  Brenda Jean Brown (4/4/1974-     ), m. 8/28/1999, Ray
             Haselhorst
36631141323  Debi Rae Brown (4/8/1975-     ), m. 12/28/1996, Steven
             Joseph Dawe (1/24/1976-    )
366311413231 Breanna Rae Dawe (9/17/1997-    )
366311413232 Ryan Joseph Dawe (6/29/1999-    )
366311413233 Cory Lee Dawe (4/20/2001-    )
366311413234 Colton James Dawe (1/14/2003-    )
36631141324  Amy Kathleen Brown (8/29/1977-    )
36631141325  Cari Marie Brown (9/11/1978-    ), m. 8/2/1996, Daniel
             James Lech (4/18/1975-    )
366311413251 Brennan Ray Lech (1/5/1997-    )
366311413252 Paiton James Lech (3/25/1998-    )
366311413253 Jacob John Lech (4/22/1999-    )
366311413254 Cali Marie Lech (4/21/2000-    )
366311413255 Regan Danielle Lech (1/7/2003-    )
36631141326  Jason Laurence Brown (9/26/1980-    )
36631141327  Megan Marguerite Brown (7/2/1982-    )
36631141328  Jodi Elaine Brown (5/8/1984-    )
36631141329  John Charles Brown (4/4/1986-12/26/1987)
3663114132x  Jamie Theresa Brown (11/29/1987-    )
3663114132a  Thomas Ryan Brown (11/1/1989-    )
3663114133   Donald Wayne Doggett (8/8/1952-    ), m. (1st) 10/25/
             1980, Phyllis Bartley Douglas Sime (12/6/1946-    ).
             M. (2nd) Linda Jo Lehman (1/25/1962-    )
             Doria Elaine Doggett (2/26/1980-    ) (Not a descendant
             . . . a child of her mother's first husband.)
36631141331  Deanna ("Deedie") Syme Doggett (3/30/1981-    )
36631141332  Adeline Danielle Doggett (6/3/2002-    )
3663114134   Marjorie Irene Doggett (6/18/1954-    ), m. 6/22/1974,
             William Jay Manning (7/17/1951-    )
36631141341  Justina Lynn Manning (10/29/1875-    ), m. 10/20/2001,
             Kevin Louis Benscoter (4/10/1981-    )
366311413411 Michael Alexander Manning (10/24/1997-    )
366311413412 Anthony Joseph Benscoter (2/24/2003-    )
3663114135   Kathleen Elaine Doggett (3/20/1957-    ), m. 4/7/1984,
             John Michael Hogmire (1/15/1956-    )
36631141351  Megan Marie Hogmire (1/22/1986-    )
36631141352  Kelci Lynn Hogmire (12/30/1988-    )
36631141353  Michela Brianne Hogmire (10/9/1994-    )
36631141354  Cody Patrick Hogmire (7/14/1996-    )
36631141355  Joel Kolbe Hogmire (8/15/1999-    )
3663114136   Raymond Eugene Doggett (8/16/1962-    ), m. 8/29/1981,
             Mary Beth Summers (7/17/1061-    )
36631141361  Terrell Lavern Doggett (8/25/1982-    ), m. Kinzey
             Teneque Zarter (2/12/1983-    )
366311413611 Keegan Ray Doggett (7/12/2003-    )
36631141362  Timothy James Doggett (1/31/1984-    )
36631141363  Matthew Lawrence Doggett (2/11/1986-    )
3663114137   Roger Dean Doggett (1/3/1966-    ), m. 5/20/1989, Tammy
             Sue Kelly
366311414    Alice Rae Doggett (3/8/1934-    ), m. 7/1/1952, Robert
             Glen Rice (2/4/1927-12/24/1991)
```

```
3663114141   Patricia Lynn Rice (6/8/1953-   ), m. 11/30/1972, David
                Scott Groves (2/15/1953-   )
36631141411  Jason Scott Groves (8/11/1974-   ), m. 11/27/1999,
                Jill Lynn Feldman (8/25/1974-   )
366311414111 Nathan Scott Groves (2/22/1998-   )
366311414112 Benjamin Allan Groves (3/8/2000-   )
36631141412  Eric Scott Groves (8/18/1980-   )
3663114142   Carolyne Jeannette Rice (7/1/1954-   ), m. 2/8/1978,
                Merwyn Ludwig (       -2/7/1979)
3663114143   Roberta Jaye Rice (4/7/1958-   ), m. (1st) Arthur
                French. M. (2nd) Lamon Marion. M. (3rd) Michael
                Fonville
36631141431  Heidi Ann French (8/31/1973-   )
366311414311 Brie Diamond French (b. and d. 6/9/1992)
36631141432  April Rae French (7/31/1980-   )
36631141433  James Austin Marion (7/22/1985-   )
3663114144   Sherri Lea Rice (3/12/1960-   ), m. 12/11/1978, James
                Curtis Petermann (4/3/1951-   )
36631141441  Joshua Andrew Petermann (9/5/1978-   )
36631141442  Natasha Lea Petermann (9/3/1981-   )
36631141443  Jennifer Evelyn Petermann (7/23/1986-   )
3663114145   Terri Jo Rice (12/1/1963-   ), m. (1st) 2/15/1981,
                Everado Lalo Gutierrez (2/15/1956-   ). M. (2nd)
                12/16/1989, Gerald Paul Dishman
36631141451  Yolanda Maria Gutierrez (4/14/1981-   )
36631141452  Angelina Alicia Gutierrez (4/4/1983-   )
36631141453  Jamie Lee Gutierrez (8/2/1985-   )
36631141454  Tyler Andrew Dishman (12/26/1992-   )
366311415    Joanne Doggett (10/25/1936-   ), m. Elmer Owens
3663114151   Greg Owens (12/8/1958-   )
36631141511  Dustin Thomas Owens (7/16/1981-   )
3663114152   Scott Owens (4/14/1960-5/19/1989)
36631141521  Elizabeth Owens (10/15/1985-   )
366311416    Robert Lea Doggett (11/29/1942-   ), m. (1st) Shirlie
                Miller. M. (2nd) Patricia Cadek (9/11/1950-   )
3663114161   Ronald Leo Doggett (8/15/1962-   ), m. Denise Scofield
36631141611  Heather Jo Doggett (10/7/1980-   )
36631141612  Rodney Lee Doggett (5/29/1983-   )
36631141613  Brooke Ann Doggett (5/20/1996-   )
3663114162   Patricia Doggett (7/25/1965-   ), m. _____ Sanderson
36631141621  Daughter
36631141622  Daughter
3663114163   Karen Doggett?, m. Edward Timmerman
3663114164   Bryan Lea Doggett (9/29/1976-   ), m. 11/1/1997, Tonya
                Marie Walker
3663114165   Anne Christine Doggett (1/7/1982-   ), m. 7/7/2001,
                Jason Eugene Underwood
366311417    Jim Alfred Doggett (4/6/1944-   ), m. 8/8/1965, Juden
                Rae Hamer (11/27/1946-   )
3663114171   Daniel Brian Doggett (6/6/1966-   ), m. (1st) 6/25/
                1988, Cynthia L. Rutten (1/16/1967-   ). M. (2nd)
                Kim Milne
36631141711  Nathan Harlow Doggett (11/17/1991-   )
```

36631141712 Dylan Paige Doggett (1/5/1995-   )
36631141713 Hayden James Doggett (10/14/2002-   )
3663114172   Teresa Ann Doggett (4/1/1968-   ), m. 8/12/1989, Brian
             Anthony Dostal (7/15/1965-   )
36631141721 Colby Paul Dostal (1/11/1993-   )
36631141722 Jordon Thomas Dostal (9/29/1995-   )
36631141723 Taylor Rose Dostal (10/26/1998-   )
366311418   Harry Allen Doggett (3/31/1947-   ), m. 1/14/1972, Delma
             Eilene Reynolds (7/14/1949-   )
3663114181   Carina ("Carrie") Lynn Doggett (9/1/1971-   ), m. 6/18/
             1993, John Carlton Brizendine (2/12/1963-   )
36631141811 Layne Carlton Brizendine (12/14/1993-   )
3663114182   Billie Jo Doggett (3/27/1977-   ), m. 7/29/2000, Freddy
             Lee ("Trey") Park III (5/6/1974-   )
36631141821 Freddy Lee ("Tracer") Park IV (5/21/2002-   )
366311419   John Dean Doggett (9/9/1952-   ), m. 6/21/1975, Cathy
             Sue Hoover (5/4/1974-   )
3663114191   Jaree Nicole Doggett (12/3/1975-   ), m. 7/21/2001,
             Sean Justin Gallagher
36631141911 Caden John Doggett (10/19/1995-   )
36631141912 Zaine Killien Maxwell Gallagher (6/19/1999-   )
36631141913 Zoe Paityn Justine Gallagher (6/2/2000-   )
3663114192   Jessica Jean Doggett (6/20/1978-   )
36631141921 Madyson Sue Doggett (10/13/1997-   )
36631142   Dolla ("Dollie") Mae Doggett (8/23/1903-2/21/1997), m.
             12/27/1928, Irwin Albert Caldwell (7/14/1902-9/2/1983)
366311421   Douglas Irwin Caldwell (5/31/1934-   ), m. 10/9/1954,
             Marilyn Jean Olsen (9/16/1936-   )
3663114211   Twigg Douglas Caldwell (7/28/1955-   ), m. 5/29/1977,
             Marguerite ("Peggy") Diane Lee (4/11/1956-   )
36631142111 Ryan Douglas Caldwell (12/31/1978-   )
36631142112 Brandon David Caldwell (12/4/1980-   )
3663114212   Elaine Eloise Caldwell (7/26/1957-   ), m. 12/23/1978,
             Robert Dale Cannon (10/2/1953-   )
36631142121 Heather Eileen Cannon (6/28/1979-   )
36631142122 Andrea Marilyn Cannon (4/13/1981-   )
36631142123 Alesha May Cannon (5/15/1985-   )
36631142124 Edward Lee Cannon (12/4/1990-   )
3663114213   Kyle James Caldwell (7/20/1959-   ), m. 8/21/1999,
             Kathleen Diane Ito (10/21/1961-   )
36631142131 Natasha Marie Caldwell (from a previous marriage)
             (3/10/1981-   ), m. 3/8/2003, Timothy Michael Cross
             (11/18/1980-   )
3663114214   Melanie May Caldwell (9/17/1962-   ), m. 5/19/1984,
             Merrick Anthony Deal (8/21/1961-   )
36631142141 Matthew Scott Deal (5/31/1987-6/1/1987)
36631142142 Megan May Deal (6/13/1988-   )
36631142143 Mackenzie Merrick Deal (6/29/1994-   )
3663114215   Holly Sue Caldwell (4/20/1964-   ), m. 11/12/1983,
             Theodore Allen Johnson (9/17/1963-   )
36631142151 Theodore Allen Johnson, Jr. (2/22/1986-   )
36631142152 Katelin Jean Johnson (3/5/1990-   )
3663115   George Grant Doggett (8/31/1875-11/28/1964), m. 11/15/
             1910, Rosetta Alice Podneore

36631151 Wayne Edward Daggett (1916-   ) (changed name from
          Doggett)
366311511 Mike Daggett
366311512 Marilyn Daggett
36631152 Daughter
3663116 John ("Dick") Morris Doggett (12/9/1877-7/16/1972), m.
          7/6/1902, Dolly Maggie Runyan
36631161 Daughter
3663117 Cary Estel Doggett (1/29/1880-6/18/1936), m. 4/2/1902,
          Lois Jeannette Moore (5/12/1881-1950)
36631171 Oris Orlue Doggett (7/20/1908-1980)
36631172 Donna Jeannette Doggett (6/27/1918-   ), m. 5/8/1947,
          Frank Dale Joachim (4/10/1912-11/5/1980)
366311721 Michael Cary Joachim (4/22/1941-5/15/1990), m. 7/25/
          1964, Karen Jean Cameron (5/31/1946-   )
3663117211 Patricia Gail Joachim (3/28/1966-   ), m. 11/18/1985,
          Dale Edward Johnson (6/13/1964-   )
36631172111 Michael David Johnson (4/24/1986-   )
36631172112 Deborah Lee Johnson (3/27/1989-   )
3663117212 Susan Marie Joachim (11/19/1970-   ), m. 6/3/1989,
          Michael Anthony Davila (5/23/1966-   )
36631172121 Cameron Cary Davila (7/21/1991-   )
36631172122 Seth Patrick Davila (6/3/1996-   )
366311722 Susan Kay Joachim (12/2/1948-   ), m. 8/25/ 1973,
          Thomas Herbert Griffith (9/21/1950-   )
3663117221 Karrie Jeannette Griffith (9/30/1974-   ), m. 12/14/
          1996, William C. Koehn (11/16/1971-   )
36631172211 Kierra Renae Koehn (12/12/1977-   )
36631172212 Kaden Thomas Koehn (2/ /2003-   )
366311723 Alan Moore Joachim (1/8/1951-   ), m. 11/19/1971,
          Vickie Marlene Klingbeil (5/16/1953-   )
3663117231 Kaycee Donna Joachim (7/18/1972-   ), m. 2/8/1992,
          Zachary Vincent Duenas (11/26/1972-   )
36631172311 Jordan Zachary Duenas (12/26/1991-2/13/1992)
36631172312 Ashliegh Victoria Duenas (5/28/1993-   )
36631172313 Austin Zachary Moore Duenas (11/17/1996-   )
3663117232 Brett Alan Joachim (9/15/1975-   ), m. 8/1/1998,
          Mindee Rae Hopkins-Hubbard (9/5/1976-   )
3663117233 Donald Philip Joachim (3/14/1977-   ), m. 2/3/2001,
          Andrea Heather Read
366311724 Dale Herbert Joachim (2/20/1952-   )
366311725 Robert Dana Joachim (9/27/1955-   ), m. 12/18/1976,
          Susan Elaine Allen (10/28/1953-   )
3663117251 Jeanette Ruth Joachim (7/14/1981-   )
3663117252 Scott Allen Joachim (8/31/1985-   )
3663117253 Rebekah Kathleen Joachim (12/15/1988-   )
36631173 Betty Jo Ann Doggett (6/4/1928-   ), m. (1st) 1946,
          _____ (deceased). M. (2nd) 5/22/1950,
          Donald William Jahns (2/23/1924-6/3/1988)
366311731 Timothy Estel Jahns (3/16/1948-   ), m. (1st) Cheryl
          Samples. M. (2nd) Connie _____
3663117311 Timothy Estel Jahns, Jr. (5/7/1971-   )
3663117312 Tami Louise Jahns (8/15/1974-   )

366311732 Donald William Jahns, Jr. (3/26/1951-11/11/1973
366311733 William Karl Jahns (10/22/1952-   ), m. 3/17/1984,
    Kimberly Ann _____
3663117331 Matthew Karl Jahns (8/29/1988-   )
366311734 Patrick Lawrence Jahns (4/1/1955-   ), m. Pamila Lynn
    Roe
3663117341 David Lawrence Jahns (10/22/1979-   )
3663117342 Jeremy Michael Jahns (5/8/1981-   )
366311735 Michael Thomas Jahns (12/4/1957-   ), m. Ruthielee
    Farrington
3663117351 Son
3663117352 Son
3663117353 Son
366311736 Mary Catherine Jahns (3/16/1961-   ), m. 9/30/1989,
    Kory Reed Heinselman
3663117361 Jacob Tad Heinselman (2/15/1991-   )
3663117362 Quinlee Catherine Heinselman (6/5/1993-   )
366311737 Barbara Ann Jahns (9/30/1965-   ), m. 9/25/1999,
    Dustin Wade Frey (1/5/1977-   )
3663117371 Jared Michael Frey (10/21/1999-   )
3663117372 Jordan Anne Frey (2/25/2003-   )
366311738 Jonathon Cary Jahns (1/22/1969-   ),m. 9/30/1993,
    Heather Jochum (6/16/1971-   )
3663117381 Sophia C. Jahns (7/10/1998-   )
3663117382 Iain C. Jahns (2/22/2001-   )
3663118 Harry Glenn Doggett (10/27/1882-6/7/1973)
3663119 Jenny Grace Doggett (7/31/1885-2/21/1945), m. (1st) 2/3/
    1903, Lafayette Lambirth. M. (2nd) 5/22/1907, George
    Frederick Young
366312 Maria Bennett (d. 12/13/1912), m. Sam Henton
366313 Jenny Bennett, m. Will Brown
36632 Charles Morris

513 Winifred Jones Eldridge (1776-before 1831), m. Rev. David
Thompson. See CORRECTIONS AND ADDITIONS page 126. "Thomson"
is correct spelling.
5131 Judith Bolling Thomson (9/18/1810-2/4/1881), m. John Gay
Bentley (4125)
5132 Thomas Eldridge Thomson, m. Blanche B.   . "Thomas"
instead of "John"
5133 Robert B. Thomson (2/8/1808-10/4/1839), m. 12/1/1831, Lillian
Ann Elizabeth Phillips (11/17/1814-6/28/1884)
51331 Winnifred Jane Thomson (10/14/1832-   ), m. 1/3/1850, John
Wesley Walker (Major, CSA) (4/14/1827-10/24/1904)
513311 John Crileas Walker (11/26/1851-12/19/1867)
513312 William Robert Walker (4/6/1855-   ), m. 11/22/1877, Mary
Elizabeth Adams (4/21/1857-4/19/1927)
5133121 Emma Agnus Walker (11/15/1878-10/2/1966), m. 9/10/1899,
William James Tyson
51331211 Lillian Mary Tyson (7/24/1900-7/4/1932), m. Morgan Smith
51331212 James Walker Tyson (11/27/1902-12/20/1903)
51331213 William Herschel Tyson (2/21/1905-4/2/1967), m. 9/10/
1937, Mable Bailey
51331214 Christine Agnus Tyson (1/25/1907-1/1/1984), m. 2/11/1927,
Paul Greening
51331215 Norma Tyson (7/24/1911-6/28/1975), m. Walter Ainsworth
51331216 Evelyn Tyson (4/17/1913-   ), m. 9/6/1936, Harold Knight
51331217 Pauline Tyson (10/22/1915-   ), m. 5/8/1938, Roy
Ainsworth
51331218 Willie Margaret Tyson (2/8/1921-   ), m. 1/4/1942,
Copeland Mobley
5133122 Bertha Jane Walker (6/27/1881-8/ /1966), m. 1/6/1901,
Walter Farmer
51331221 Ben Farmer
51331222 Curtis Farmer
51331223 Mable Farmer
51331224 William Farmer
51331225 Annette Farmer
5133123 John Thomson Walker (8/14/1883-7/12/1916), m. 5/13/1907,
Minnie Nash
51331231 Temple Walker
51331232 Marshall Walker
51331233 Mary Ann Walker
51331234 Christine Walker
5133124 Lillie Elizabeth Walker (1/11/1886-3/16/1986), m. G. M.
Jones
5133125 Augustus Adams Walker (7/10/1888-4/10/1889)
5133126 William Edward Walker (1/31/1890-2/7/1977), m. 7/4/1919,
Shirley Wright
5133127 Robert Victor Walker (8/1/1892-   ), m. 12/ /1921,
Audilea Adams
5133128 Lewis Paul Walker (10/12/1894-7/17/1938), m. 7/24/1914,
Margie Emma Jane Fuller (9/26/1896-11/30/1953)
51331281 Jo Eloise Walker (5/8/1915-   ), m. 7/25/1936, Kenneth
Vardell Stewart
513312811 Mary Eloise Stewart (9/11/1937-   ), m. 1/26/1958,
Dick Richardson (6/10/1930-   )

5133128111 Dick Stewart Richardson (8/23/1958-   ), m. 10/7/1978,
            Stephanie Tackett (7/10/1959-   )
51331281111 Ashley Lee Richardson (9/26/1979-   )
51331281112 Amber Nicole Richardson (3/12/1982-   )
513312812   Paula Kay Stewart (1/7/1939-10/22/1959), m. 8/17/1958,
            John Donald Durham
5133128121 John Michael Durham (10/22/1959-   ), m. 7/20/1991,
            Tonya Ann Woods (9/25/1963-   )
513312813   Robert Lance Stewart (11/9/1942-   ), m. (1st) 5/12/
            1970, Jo Ann Smith (2/8/1946-   ); m. (2nd) 10/3/
            1987, Velita Womble
5133128131 Melanie Elena Stewart (5/3/1974-   )
51331282   Verus Elizabeth Walker (10/10/1922-   ), m. 7/4/1942,
            John Pleasant Honaker III (7/31/1921-   )
513312821   William Allen Honaker (3/10/1943-3/10/1943)
513312822   John Pleasant Honaker IV (9/8/1944-   ), m. 6/2/1969,
            Virginia Charlene Griner (6/17/1949-   )
5133128221 John Pleasant Honaker V (9/6/1970-   )
5133128222 Charles Henry Honaker (1/2/1975-   )
513312823   Robert Lewis Honaker (9/22/1946-   ), m. 4/22/1967,
            Sandra Lynn Hall (10/4/1947-   )
5133128231 Robin Lynn Honaker (12/26/1969-   ), m. Mohamed Arab
51331282311 Mariam Nashida Arab (1/6/1991-   )
51331282312 Abraham Arab (5/17/1992-   )
513312824   Kenneth Don Honaker (3/4/1953-   ), m. (2nd) 2/28/1976,
            Brenda Batson (1/6/1952-   )
5133128241 Kenneth Don Honaker II (9/11/1979-   )
5133128242 Christopher Vernon Honaker (8/3/1982-   )
51331283   William Robert Walker (2/14/1925-   ), m. 6/6/1947,
            Janette Barnum (12/30/1927-   )
513312831   Cynthia Dean Walker (7/12/1950-   ), m. 8/24/1968,
            Robert Glynn Wells (9/22/1947-   )
5133128311 Chad Steven Wells (4/21/1969-   ), m. (1st) 8/26/
            1989,Charlsye Johnette Mann (8/8/1970-   ); m. (2nd)
            2/ /2003, Tamey Anderson
5133128312 Jason Glynn Wells (2/20/1971-   ), m. 10/10/1990,
            Julie Kay Lum (1/1/1973-   )
51331283121 Lauren Michelle Wells (5/22/1991-   ) (twin)
51331283122 Lindsay Renee Wells (5/22/1991-   ) (twin)
51331283123 Tanner Glynn Wells (4/15/1998-   )
513312832   Judith Sue Walker (9/26/1956-   ), m. 9/28/1974, Mark
            Gentry (3/1/1955-   )
5133128321 Robert Walker Gentry (4/24/1976-   )
5133128322 Melissa Sue Gentry (8/8/1979-   ), m. (1st) Don Allen
            McCoy; m. (2nd) Rogelio Moreno, Jr.
51331283221 Joshua Allen Gentry (11/28/1995-   )
51331283222 Stephen Anthony Moreno (7/7/1998-   )
5133128323 John Mark Gentry (7/14/1982-   ), m. 8/15/1902, Sara
            Elaine Cox
51331283231 Celeste Isabella Lay (5/16/2002-   ), adopted by
            Todd & Diane Lay
51331284   Doris Dean Walker (10/4/1926-   ), m. 2/17/1945, Charles
            Robert Harlan (3/30/1923-   )

513312841 Elizabeth Louise Harlan (12/2/1946-   ), m. (1st) 3/18/
      1966, Donald M. Daray; m. (2nd) 9/22/1972, John F.
      Twardowski
5133128411 John Robert Daray (10/1/1966-   ), m. 11/12/1988,
      Jennifer Cantron
5133128412 Elizabeth Anne Twardowski (5/16/1974-   )
513312842 Margie Ann Harlan (5/29/1952-   ), m. (1st) 3/14/1971,
      Peter Shaffer; m. (2nd) 5/31/1975, Charles Roznovak;
      m. (3rd) 12/16/1988, Peter Yang (7/13/1951-   )
5133128421 Matthew Ryan Roznovak (7/8/1980-   )
5133128422 Meghan Lindsey Roznovak (4/13/1983-   )
5133128423 Emily Lauren Yang (1/8/1990-   )
5133128424 Kate Lian Yang (5/18/1991-   )
513312843 Mary Virginia Harlan (9/16/1954-   ), m. 5/31/1986,
      Roger Lynn Boltz (7/17/1948-   )
5133128431 Travis Harlan Boltz (10/3/1990-   )
51331285 Lewis Paul Walker, Jr. (1/19/1928-7/15/1972), m. (8/22/
      1946, Mary Ann Driggers (5/4/1929-   )
513312851 Betty Carol Walker (8/13/1947-   ), m. (1st) James
      Patrick Miller; m. (2nd) 6/7/1969, Herman Lee Tipton
      (1/1/1947-   )
5133128511 Paul Wesley Tipton (9/23/1970-   ), m. 1993, Deena
      Lynn McDaniel
51331285111 Chad Wesley Tipton (11/21/1993-   )
51331285112 Ryan Tipton (6/ /1996-   )
5133128512 John Lewis Tipton (1/2/1973-   )
5133128513 Kristen Tipton (6/29/1974-   ), m. 6/8/1994, Robert
      Todd Shugart
51331285131 Taylor Elizabeth Shugart (12/8/1995-   )
51331285132 Ashleigh Shugart (/ /2001-   )
513312852 Paula Catherine Walker (6/24/1948-   ), m. 8/15/1970,
      Rev. Michael Dulaney Chalk (12/23/1947-   )
5133128521 Brian David Chalk (12/6/1973-   )
5133128522 Mary Catherine Chalk (3/27/1976-   )
513312853 Donna Louise Walker (7/12/1949-   ), m. 5/15/1971,
      Howard Burton Eddins III (11/13/1947-   )
5133128531 Amy Catherine Eddins (9/7/1973-   )
5133128532 Sunny Elizabeth Eddins (3/22/1976-   ), m. 3/7/1998,
      Richard Riley Haddock
51331285321 Johnathan Ross Eddins (11/22/1996-   )
51331285322 Joshua Burton Haddock (3/31/1998-   )
51331285323 Marianne Ruth Haddock (5/11/2000-   )
5133128533 Melissa Day Eddins (12/3/1982-   )
513312854 Jeannie Lynn Walker (10/3/1951-   ), m. 4/17/1970,
      Allan David Cavender (4/23/1952-   )
5133128541 Allan David Cavender, Jr. (1/1/1971-   )
5133128542 Melanie Ann Cavender (9/7/1972-   )
51331286 Roma Nell Walker (5/27/1930-   ), m. 1/21/1948, Paul De
      La Croix (11/2/1925-   )
513312861 Cherie De La Croix (11/4/1948-   ), m. Albert Wayne
      Daigle (9/2/1947-   )
5133128611 Amie Claire Daigle (9/15/1971-   ), m. 11/ /1998,
      Robert Stassi
51331286111 Benjamin Robert Stassi (5/1/2003-   )

```
5133128612  Emilie Lauren Daigle (4/4/1974-    ), m. 7/19/2003,
            Troy Archer
5133128613  Meg Catherine Daigle (1/9/1976-   )
5133128614  Ellen Elizabeth Daigle (3/9/1978-   )
513312862   Denise De La Croix (1/26/1951-    ), m. 8/16/1973, Larry
            Keith Daigle (5/29/1950-   )
5133128621  Jamison Fuller Daigle (8/7/1977-   )
5133128622  Sarah Elizabeth Daigle (9/11/1980-   )
513312863   Charles Paul De La Croix (1/14/1954-    ), m. 9/1/1995,
            Jane Schmidt
5133128631  Alexander Paul De La Croix (7/3/1997-   )
5133128632  Darren Charles De La Croix (1/30/1999-   )
513312864   Suzonne De La Croix (8/17/1957-    ), m. 3/15/1980,
            Keith Wayne Bourque (3/7/1957-   )
5133128641  Katie Elizabeth Bourque (9/5/1983-   )
5133128642  Hannah Elizabeth Bourque (11/2/1987-   )
513312865   Deidre De La Croix (10/22/1962-    ), m. (1st) 6/23/1984,
            George B. Holstead III (2/26/1962-    ); m. (2nd) 1992,
            James Macklen
5133128651  George Burnham Holstead IV (12/6/1990-   )
5133128652  Mary Kathryn Macklen (11/6/1992-   )
51331287    Curtis Don Walker (7/24/1933-7/12/1998), m. 9/5/1954,
            Maggie Faye Norred (11/18/1934-   )
513312871   Ronda Faye Walker (6/9/1955-    ), m. 8/3/1974, Paul
            Lindsay Sadler (4/29/1955-   )
5133128711  Erin Michele Sadler (10/29/1975-   )
5133128712  Brandon Lindsay Sadler (4/6/1982-   )
513312872   Curtis Don Walker, Jr. (11/14/1958-    ), m. 6/5/1983,
            Nancy Kay Nelson (11/14/1960-   )
5133128721  Julius Tate Walker (9/19/1985-   )
5133128722  Maria Danielle Walker (8/14/1992-   )
5133128723  Jared Layton Walker (9/14/1994-   )
513312873   Mary Elizabeth Walker (5/19/1962-    ), m. 11/9/1984,
            Tommy Ray Russell (7/22/1959-   )
5133128731  Christopher Walker Russell (10/10/1986-   )
5133128732  Jeremy Ray Russell (9/15/1987-   )
5133128733  Sarah Elizabeth Russell (4/11/1995-   )
5133129     George Francis Walker (2/9/1897-6/ /1974), m. 6/18/1923,
            Letha Kelly
513313      Lillie Jones Walker (4/21/1856-5/30/1953), m. 11/19/1874,
            Robert Wyley Wright
5133131     Howard Walker Wright (11/2/1875-12/12/1967)
5133132     Crileas Eustace Wright (6/11/1878-died at 18 months)
5133133     Henry Hugh Wright (6/21/1880- / /1935)
5133134     Robert Errett Wright (1/28/1884- / /1896)
5133135     Sam Wright (11/12/1885-11/4/1973)
5133136     Grace Winifred Wright (4/28/1888-   )
5133137     Tom Jones Wright (2/3/1892-7/14/1921)
513314      Kate Walker (4/17/1858-    ), m. 12/ /1880, Frank W. Broach
5133141     Alice Broach
5133142     Lilly Broach
5133143     Norman Broach
5133144     Gay Broach
5133145     Winnifred ("Winnie") Broach
```

5133146 Kate Broach
5133147 May Broach
5133148 Robert Broach
5133149 Lucille Broach
513315   Sallie Walker (3/24/1860-3/21/1861)
513316   Ruth Walker (10/29/1867-3/7/1955), m. 2/12/1890, Mastin
         Leonidas Northum
5133161 Rachel Christine Northum
5133162 Elijah Homer Northum
5133163 Winifred Northum
5133164 Naida Northum
51332   Thomas David Thomson (11/8/1834-   ), m. Martha A. Cross
51333   Nathaniel Terry Thomson (7/7/1836-7/17/1839)
51334   George Warren Thomson (5/27/1838-10/18/1865)
5134   (Daughter) Thomson, m. William E. Johnson
5135   John W. Thomson
5136   William H. Thomson

         Second child of first husband:

5155   William Hill (1809-ca. 1839), m. Betsy Steger (ca. 1813-   ),
       dau. of Peyton and Frances Jefferson Steger (Cumberland
       County, VA).
51551 Thomas J. Hill (9/9/1828-4/3/1883). B. Alabama, d. Caldwell
       County, TX)
51552 Edward Peyton Hill (6/10/1833-1/16/1916). B. Alabama, d.
       Caldwell County, TX. M. (1st) Margaret Davidson, m. (2nd)
       1868, Mary Ann Leovell (1847-1909)
       Children by first wife:
515521 Jimmie Davidson Hill (1853-1884), m. Minnie Neill (1866-
       1947)
515522 Edward Peyton Hill, Jr. (1865-1969), m. Henrietta Louisa
       McGinnis (1870-1969)
       Children by second wife:
515523 Dempse Dekalb Hill (9/15/1870-7/21/1944)
515524 Thomas Steger Hill (12/11/1871-12/31/1944)
515525 William Columbus Hill (4/3/1875-6/15/1932). B. Caldwell
       County, TX
515526 John Leovell Hill (7/8/1877-3/7/1958)
515527 Van McBride Hill (8/8/1879-6/3/1960)
515528 Harriett Melissa Hill (6/1/1881-4/30/1965)
515529 Marvin Collier Hill (8/15/1885-5/5/1970)
51552x James Louise Hill (8/15/1885-5/5/1970)
51552a Howard Hassie Hill (6/3/1887-6/28/1977), m. 12/8/1907, in
       Bell County, TX, Jessie Lee McGinnis (6/22/1892-12/4/1981)
51552a1 Daryl (Darrell) Barton Hill (3/20/1910-5/20/1991). B. San
       Marcos, TX., d. Salem, AR. M. 4/4/1933, in San Marcos,
       TX, DeEtta Jewell Byler
51552a2 Edward Peyton Hill (4/21/1913-5/6/1065). B. in Caldwell
       County, TX, d. in Galveston, TX. M. 6/22/1935 in Bell
       County, TX, Billie Louise Sloan (8/21/1918 in Lampasas
       County, TX-   ), dau. of Dougan and Willie Smith
       Sloan.

51552a21 Howard Wayne Hill (5/9/1937-6/25/1993). B. in Bell
County, TX, d. in Brazoria County, TX. M. 12/22/1956,
in Brazoria County, TX, Marie Greenawalt (11/6/1938-   )
B. in Houston, TX, dau. of Millard and Maudis Felder
Greenawalt.

51552a211 Pamela Ruth Hill (9/26/1957-   ). B. in Brazoria
County, TX. M. 11/6/1981, in Brazoria County, TX,
Morris Taylor Massingill (10/14/1955-   ). B. in
Brazoria County, TX

51552a2111 Justin Taylor Massingill (11/26/1982-   ). B. in
Harris County, TX

51552a2112 Jordan Thomas Massingill (7/15/1984-   ). B. in
Harris County, TX

51552a212 Glenn Howard Hill (10/23/1959-   ). B. in Brazoria
County, TX. M. 5/9/1981, in Brazoria, TX, Beverly
Renee Huber (1/17/1961-   ). Div. 1995 or 1996.

51552a2121 Rebecca Renee Hill (11/20/1981-   ). B. in Brazoria
County, TX

51552a2122 Marissa Nicole Hill (10/1/1990-5/30/1995). B. in
Brazoria County, TX, d. in Harris County, TX

51552a213 Jon Wayne Hill (5/21/1961-   ). B. in Brazoria County,
TX, m. 3/5/1994, in Brazoria County, TX, Lorraine Marie
VanDyk Hicks (8/21/1958-   )

51552a22 Billy Joe Hill (8/22/1941-   ). B. Bell County, TX.
M. 4/30/1965, in Brazoria County, TX, Beatrice Marie
Labay (11/4/1943 in Wharton County, TX-   ), dau. of
Jerome and Emma Smaistrla LaBay.

51552a221 Tracy Marie Hill (9/20/1973-   ). B. in San Patricio
County, TX

51552a222 Courtney Lynn Hill (10/7/1982-   ). B. in Brazoria
County, TX

51552a23 Joyce Ann Hill (9/23/1943-   ). B. in Comal County,
TX. M. 1/31/1970, in Brazoria County, TX, Raymond Lee
Rives (12/8/1943-   ). B. in Brazoria County, TX

51552a231 Jeanne Renee Ruston (3/25/1961-   )

51552a2311 Steven Cole Ruston (7/5/1983-   ). B. in Brazoria
County, TX

51552a232 Jennifer Dianne Ruston (6/2/1962-   ). B. in Brazoria
County, TX. M. 8/22/1987, in Brazoria County, TX, Scott
Dunlap (10/22/1961-   )

51552a233 Susan Lea Rives (9/23/1970-   ). B. in Brazoria County,
TX

51552a24 James Edward Hill (1/17/1948-   ). B. in Brazoria
County, TX. M. 7/30/1971, in Brazoria County, TX,
Sandra Kay Hudson

Note: Adopted children of James Edward Hill and Sandra Kay
Hudson:
(a) Ronald Dwayne Hill (7/18/1968-   ), m. 1/5/2002, in
FL, Jennifer Rae Jones.
(b) William Allen Hill (7/11/1970-   )

51552a241 James Peyton Hill (8/2/1973-   ), m. 9/28/1996, in
Brazoria County, TX, Jennifer Wendell

51552a2411 Dillon Peyton Hill (9/ /2001-   )

51552a3   Doris Wilden Hill (6/17/1918-3/ /11997). B. Caldwell
          County, TX, d. Cherokee County, TX. M. 11/25/1933,
          Arthur Moran Cox (1912-1983)
51552a4   William Royce Hill (2/19/1922-7/8/1976). B. Caldwell
          County, TX, d. Oxford, AR. M. 9/16/1928, in Hays
          County, TX, Evelyn Grace Nichols
51552a41 Kathy Hill (8/5/1949-   ). B. Hays County, TX. M.
          David White
51552a42 Christy Ann Hill (9/26/1952-   ). B. Calico Rock, AR
51552a43 William Royce Hill, Jr. (9/27/1955-   ). B. Calico
          Rock, AR. M. Diane Sawyer (1/ /1956-   )
51553   John I. Hill
51554   Sarah F. Hill

573 Martha ("Patsy") Rives (d. 1829), m. John Wilkinson who served
     in 4th Co. 3rd Rgt., Va

5736 Henry Benjamin Wilkinson, a soldier, 39th Va. Militia, War of
      1812 of sussex County, m. Ann Elizabeth Kirkland of Sussex
      County

57362 Martha Frances Wilkinson (6/ /1832-1/25/1894) of Sussex
       County, m. 6/4/1851, Chastine Herod Talley (1831-6/11/1899)
       of Petersburg, a soldier, 18th Va. Inf. Rgt., CSA, son of
       Randolph Peyton and Martha Crowder Talley of Amelia County
573621   William Henry Talley (7/4/1853-3/9/1929) of Petersburg, m.
         1/26/1898, Margaret Slaughter Atkins (1/7/1873-3/8/1965),
         dau. of Andrew B. and Laura Slaughter Atkins of Petersburg
5736211 William Henry Talley, Jr. (12/7/1898-11/3/1971) of Peters-
         burg, m. 6/9/1928, Audrey Beatrice Hurt (2/2/1897-5/5/
         1967), dau. of Herbert L. and Elizabeth Edwards Hurt of
         Crewe, VA
57362111 William Henry Talley III (2/9/1929-   ) of Petersburg,
          m. 12/20/1952, Betty Fay White (3/22/1930-   ) of
          Richmond, dau. of George Melvin and Ethel Stirling White
          of Richmond
573621111 William Henry Talley IV (5/5/1955-   ) of Petersburg,
           m. 8/12/1978, Margaret Elizabeth Baskervill of South
           Boston, VA, dau. of William Nelson and Julia Moore
           Baskervill of South Boston
5736211111 William Henry Talley V (6/26/1981-   ) of Petersburg
5736211112 Elizabeth Baskervill Talley (5/11/1984-   ) of
            Petersburg
5736211113 Andrew Atkins Talley (8/17/1989-   ) of Petersburg
573621112 Lisa Stirling Talley (11/11/1956-   ) of Petersburg,
           m. 9/10/1988, Arnold Borden McKinnon, Jr. (12/18/1953-
) of Chevy Chase, MD, son of Arold B. and
           Orianna McArthur McKinnon of Norfolk, VA
5736211121 Arnold Borden McKinnon III (12/10/1990-   ) (twin)
            of Chevy Chase
5736211122 Anna Stirling McKinnon (12/10/1990-   ) (twin) of
            Chevy Chase
573621113 Melvin White Talley (5/22/1960-   ) of Petersburg
573621114 Kathryn Paul Talley (6/1/1967-   ) of Petersburg

57362112 Audrey Hurt Talley (5/1/1934-   ) of Petersburg, m.
          1/18/1951, James Lee Dean, Jr. (11/10/1930-   ) of
          Petersburg
573621121 Patricia Lynn Dean (5/8/1953-   ) of Petersburg, m.
          William C. Rohde (3/23/1946-   ) of Maryland
5736211211 Jennifer Marie Rohde (3/15/1976-   ) of Colonial
          Heights, VA
5736211212 Kristin Jennette Rohde (7/28/1981-   ) of Colonial
          Heights
573621122 James Lee Dean III (10/31/1057-   ) of Colonial Heights
5736212   Martha Atkins Talley (9/23/1900-12/12/1983) of Petersburg,
          m. Russell C. Youngblood (1/23/1895-2/8/1959) of Prince
          George County, a soldier, Sgt. U.S. Army, WIA, World
          War I
5736213   Virginia May Talley (4/15/1903-1/3/1946) of Petersburg, m.
          Leslie A. Parker (1900-   ) of Virginia

573622   Alice Elizabeth Talley (9/5/1855-   ) of Petersburg, m.
          6/10/1874, Charles Alexander Slaughter (8/31/1854-
          4/7/1929), son of John J. and Martha Ledbetter Slaughter
          of Petersburg

57363   Rebecca Jane Wilkinson (1837-3/30/1910) of Sussex County, m.
          Thomas J. Gates (11/26/1832-5/25/1893) of Petersburg
57364   Henry Thomas Wilkinson (1839-5/5/1864) of Sussex County,
          1st Lt., 22nd Bn. Va. Inf., CSA, KIA
57365   Rufus Allen Wilkinson (2/21/1840-3/18/1912) of Sussex
          County, a soldier, 22nd Bn. Va. Inf., CSA, m. 10/8/1867,
          Martha Jefferson Slaughter (5/24/1849-6/12/1903) of Peters-
          burg, dau. of John J. and Martha Ledbetter Slaughter of
          Petersburg
573651   Charles Lee Wilkinson (7/1/1071-5/10/1946) of Petersburg,
          m. Mary Anna Tate (5/17/1878-1/11/1949) of Orange County
5736511   Gladys Elizabeth Wilkinson (3/28/1908-   ) of Petersburg
          and by profession a public school teacher in Petersburg

641732   Natalie Page Coleman (b. in Halifax County, d. 1/17/1961, in Richmond), m. George MacLaren Brydon (b. in Danville, d. 9/26/1963, in Richmond)

6417321   George MacLaren Brydon, Jr. (d. 1970, in Richmond), m. Cleland Harris (6/10/1901, in Georgetown, SC - 7/5/1994, in Richmond)

64173211 Cleland Page Brydon (b. in Richmond), m. Leveson Gower Leslie, Jr. (7/14/1930, in Danville-   )

641732111 Edith Page Leslie (8/28/1953, in Charlottesville-), m. Torquil MacCorkle, Jr. (9/ /1955, in Lexington-   )

6417321111 Sara Lyons MacCorkle (2/ /1984-   )

6417321112 Torquil MacCorkle III (6/18/1986-   )

6417321113 Kristen Page MacCorkle (7/2/1990-   )

641732112 Evelyn Byrd Leslie (9/1/1955, in Fredericksburg-), m. Jeffrey Warner Swallen (3/12/1951, in Evanston, IL-)

6417321121 Peter Leslie Swallen (4/2/1986, in Richmond-   )

6417321122 Richard MacLaren Swallen (4/11/1989, in Richmond-)

641732113 Stephen Gower Leslie (4/23/1962, in Alexandria-   )

641732114 Lindsay MacLaren Leslie (10/23/1965, in Alexandria- 5/ /1996, in Richmond)

64173212 Carter Randolph Brydon (d. 1980), m. John Williamson Moore III

641732121 Cleland Randolph Moore (1964-   ), m. Mark Patrick Murray-Thriepland (b. in Scotland)

6417321211 Mary Carter Murray-Thriepland (2001-   )

641732122 Taylor Nelson Moore (1969-   ), m. John Doty Alexander

6417321221 Natalie Alexander

6417321222 Henry Wolf Alexander (2001-   )

64173213 David MacLaren Brydon (d. after 1996, in plane crash near Kotzebue, Alaska

6417322   Anne Page Brydon (7/29/1904, in Hamilton, VA-   )

6417323   Robert Brydon III, m. Jean Whittet Wood (d. 1987, in Richmond)

64173231 Robert Carter Brydon, m. (1st) Evelyn Christian; m. (2nd) Mary Bullard

641732311 Carter Christian Brydon (1963-   ), m. Paige Miller

6417323111 Miller Chadwick Brydon (7/12/1997-)

64173232 Jean Wood Brydon (11/2/1939-   )

6417324   Nathaniel Coleman Brydon, m. Grace Langhorne Slater (b. in Redlands, CA - 5/16/1995, in Richmond)

64173241 Nathaniel Coleman Brydon, Jr., m. Joy DeShazor

641732411 John Coleman Brydon (1980-   )

641732412 Susanna Sinclair Brydon (1983-   )

64173242 George MacLaren Brydon III (1946-   ), m. Katherine Hindrelet

641732421 George MacLaren Brydon IV (1975-   )

64173243 Sally Slater Brydon (1949-   ), m.Stephen B.Booth

641732431 Edward Alvey Booth (1984-   )

641732432 William Brydon Booth (1987-   )

On pages 300 and 301, items 641733 through 641739 have been omitted. Items 641733, 641734, 641735, 641736, 641737, 641738 and 641739 are not descendants of Nathaniel Ragsdale Coleman (64173). They are descendants of Carter Page (244) and his second wife Lucy Nelson.

In order to properly show this omission, the omitted numbers are listed here and will be indexed.

641733 Robert Brydon, Jr. (12/1/1876-), m. 5/3/1905, Olive
    Pearl Guerrant (4/2/1880-), dau. of Joseph Bascom and
    Lizzie Frances Osborne Guerrant
6417331 Earl Guerrant Brydon (8/24/1906-), m. 6/26/1932, Willa
    Mae Williams (6/8/1909-), dau. of Thomas Henry and
    Eliza Marie White Williams
64173311 Patricia Page Brydon (3/2/1936-7/15/1937)
64173312 Robert Earl Brydon (12/10/1938-)
64173313 Elizabeth Ilane Brydon (1/12/1941-)
6417332 Ellen Page Brydon (1/6/1915-)
641734 Mary Evelyn Brydon, M.D. (6/2/1878-4/13/1930), m. 9/5/1925,
    George Ladeen Mackay (2/13/1857-), son of Daniel and
    Margaret Deacon Mackay of Scotland
641735 Ellen Dane Brydon (12/13/1879-), m. 10/4/1910, William
    Edgar Murrie (9/30/1871-), son of McAden and Laura
    Martha Flippen Murrie
6417351 Robert Brydon Murrie (8/28/1911-). Unm.
6417352 Laura Flippen Murrie (1/30/1913-), m. 8/30/1936,
    William Clyde Rodgers (8/16/1913-), son of William
    Clyde and Florina Humphreys Rodgers
64173521 Laura Humphreys Rodgers (9/21/1937-)
64173522 Ellon Dame Rodgers (7/15/1943-)
6417353 Ellen Dame Murrie (10/6/1915-)
6417354 William Edgar Murrie (10/6/1917-6/7/1919)
6417355 Hilda MacLaren Murrie (8/19/1920-)
641736 Carter Page Brydon (5/1/1881-), m. 12/10/1919, Minnie
    Nunley (widow of Raymond Levin Holt) (12/7/1885-),
    dau. of William P. and Ella Swain Nunley. No issue.
641737 Margaret Page Brydon (9/11/1883-5/31/1942). Unm.
641738 Lucy Nelson Brydon (7/6/1886-). Unm.
641739 Nona Irving Brydon (5/8/1889-7/5/1889)

INDEX

NOTE: The name of the spouse of a Pocahontas descendant is indexed even though that spouse is not a descendant of Pocahontas, but the name of a parent of such a spouse is not indexed unless, of course, that parent is a descendant of Pocahontas.

Byler, DeEtta Jewell 51552a1
Byrd, Susan Lewis 3231
Byrd, William Powel 3231

C

Cabell, Sophonisba E. 1321
Cable, Deborah 3663113244
Cadek, Patricia 366311416
Caldwell, Brandon David 36631142112
Caldwell, Dolla ("Dollie") Mae Doggett 36631142
Caldwell, Douglas Irwin 366311421
Caldwell, Elaine Eloise 3663114212
Caldwell, Holly Sue 3663114215
Caldwell, Irwin Albert 36631142
Caldwell, Kathleen Diane Ito 3663114213
Caldwell, Kyle James 3663114213
Caldwell, Marguerite ("Peggy") Diane Lee 3663114211
Caldwell, Marilyn Jean Olsen 366311421
Caldwell, Melanie May 3663114214
Caldwell, Natasha Marie 36631142131
Caldwell, Ryan Douglas 36631142111
Caldwell, Twigg Douglas 3663114211
Cameron, Karen Jean 366311721
Cannon, Alesha May 36631142123
Cannon, Andrea Marilyn 36631142122
Cannon, Edward Lee 36631142124
Cannon, Elaine Eloise Caldwell 3663114212
Cannon, Heather Eileen 36631142121
Cannon, Robert Dale 3663114212
Cantron, Jennifer 5133128411
Cavender, Allan David 513312854
Cavender, Allan David, Jr. 5133128541
Cavender, Jeannie Lynn Walker 513312854
Cavender, Melanie Ann 5133128542
Chalk, Brian David 5133128521
Chalk, Mary Catherine 5133128522
Chalk, Paula Catherine Walker 513312852
Chalk, Rev. Michael Dulaney 513312852
Chartier, Sheila Gail 3663113241
Christian, Evelyn 64173231
Clover, Betty 3663112331
Clover, Cheryl 3663112331
Clover, Jason 36631123313
Clover, John F. II 366311233
Clover, John F. III 3663112331
Clover, John F. IV 36631123312
Clover, Mary L. Bowlyow 366311233
Clover, Tammy 36631123311
Coleman, Natalie Page 641732
Coleman, Nathaniel Ragsdale 64173
Connery, Ellen Lynn 3663113242
Cox, Arthur Moran 51552a3
Cox, Doris Wilden Hill 51552a3
Cox, Sara Elaine 5133128323
Crosby, Erma Colleen 366311412
Cross, Martha A. 51332
Cross, Natasha Marie Caldwell 36631142131
Cross, Timothy Michael 36631142131

D

Daggett (Doggett), Wayne Edward 36631151
Daggett, Edith 36631112
Daggett, Ella Mae 36631113
Daggett, Ida Mahalia Marks 3663111
Daggett, Isaac ("Ike") Bennett 3663111
Daggett, Marilyn 366311512
Daggett, Mike 366311511
Daggett, Opal 36631111
Daggett, Warren LeRoy 36631114
Daigle, Albert Wayne 513312861
Daigle, Amie Claire 5133128611
Daigle, Cherie De La Croix 513312861
Daigle, Denise De La Croix 513312862
Daigle, Ellen Elizabeth 5133128614
Daigle, Emilie Lauren 5133128612
Daigle, Jamison Fuller 5133128621
Daigle, Larry Keith 513312862
Daigle, Meg Catherine 5133128613
Daigle, Sarah Elizabeth 5133128622
Dandridge, Bettie Bolling 17114
Dandridge, Bolling Starke 1711
Dandridge, Charles S. 17116
Dandridge, Elizabeth Ann Bowles 1711
Dandridge, Julia C. 17113
Dandridge, Laura 17111
Dandridge, Lucy M 17112
Dandridge, Sarah ("Sallie") 17117 ,
Dandridge, Thomasia L. 17115
Daray, Donald M. 513312841
Daray, Elizabeth Louise Harlan 513312841
Daray, Jennifer Cantron 5133128411
Daray, John Robert 5133128411
Davidson, Margaret 51552
Davies, Coral Synnott 219361311
Davies, Hugh Jonathan Edward 219361311
Davies, Hugh Walter 21936131
Davies, Josephine Peppett Bolling 219361
Davies, Lt. Commander Hugh M. 2193613
Davies, Mark Timothy 219361312
Davies, Patricia Helen Kease 21936131
Davila, Cameron Cary 36631172121
Davila, Michael Anthony 3663117212
Davila, Seth Patrick 36631172122
Davila, Susan Marie Joachim 3663117212
Dawe, Breanna Rae 366311413231
Dawe, Colton James 366311413234
Dawe, Cory Lee 366311413233
Dawe, Debi Rae Brown 36631141323
Dawe, Ryan Joseph 366311413232
Dawe, Steven Joseph 36631141323
De La Croix, Alexander Paul 5133128631
De La Croix, Charles Paul 513312863
De La Croix, Cherie 513312861
De La Croix, Darren Charles 5133128632
De La Croix, Deidre 513312865
De La Croix, Denise 513312862
De La Croix, Jane Schmidt 513312863
De La Croix, Paul 51331286
De La Croix, Roma Nell Walker 51331286

De La Croix, Suzonne 513312864
Deal, Mackenzie Merrick 36631142143
Deal, Matthew Scott 36631142141
Deal, Megan May 36631142142 .
Deal, Melanie May Caldwell 3663114214
Deal, Merrick Anthony 3663114214
Dean, Audrey Hurt Talley 57362112
Dean, James Lee, Jr. 57362112
Dean, James Lee III 573621122
Dean, Patricia Lynn 573621121
DeMiller, Colonel 132116
DeMiller, Hebe Carter Grayson 132116
Dennis, Bertha Watson 1321154
Dennis, John Stanley 1321154
DeRham, Estelle Randolph Bolling Austen 2193611
DeRham, Henry Longfellow 2193611
DeShazor, Joy 64173241
Dishman, Gerald Paul 3663114145
Dishman, Terry Jo Rice Gutierrez 3663114145
Dishman, Tyler Andrew 36631141454
Dixon, Capt. ("Captain Hal") Henry Dixon 132112
Dixon, Mary Eleanor Grayson 132112
Dixon, Mona 36631124
Dixon, Susan 13211
Doggett (daughter) 36631152
Doggett (daughter) 36631161
Doggett, Adeline Danielle 36631141332
Doggett, Alice Margaret Austin 3663114
Doggett, Alice Rae 366311414
Doggett, Anne Christine 3663114165
Doggett, Arminda Lucille Lester 3663114124
Doggett, Benjamin William 36631141235
Doggett, Betty Jo Ann 36631173
Doggett, Beverly Jean 3663114132
Doggett, Billie Jo 3663114182
Doggett, Brett Russell 3663114125
Doggett, Brooke Ann 36631141613
Doggett, Bryan Lea 3663114164
Doggett, Caden John 36631141911
Doggett, Candice Ann 36631141133
Doggett, Carina ("Carrie") Lynn 3663114181
Doggett, Cary Armstead 366311
Doggett, Cary Estel 3663117
Doggett, Casey Joe 3663114114
Doggett, Casey Ryan 36631141233
Doggett, Cathy Sue Hoover 366311419
Doggett, Cheryl Ann Madson 3663114123
Doggett, Cody Bryan 36631141243
Doggett, Cynthia L. Rutten 3663114171
Doggett, Daniel Brian 3663114171
Doggett, Darla Ramstad 3663114126
Doggett, Deanna ("Deedie") Syme 36631141331
Doggett, Delma Eilene Reynolds 366311418
Doggett, Denise Scofield 3663114161
Doggett, Dick Laurence 366311413
Doggett, Dolla ("Dollie") Mae 3663114142
Doggett, Dolly Maggie Runyan 3663116
Doggett, Donald Wayne 3663114133

Doggett, Donna Jeannette 36631172
Doggett, Douglas 36631141142
Doggett, Dusty Lee 36631141132
Doggett, Dylan Paige 36631141712
Doggett, Elaine Alvera Simons 366311413
Doggett, Erma Colleen Crosby 366311412
Doggett, Ethan 36631141141
Doggett, Gale James 366311412
Doggett, George Grant 3663115
Doggett, Gerald Laurence 3663114131
Doggett, Gloria Kay 3663114115
Doggett, Harlow Harry 36631141
Doggett, Harry Allen 366311418
Doggett, Harry Glenn 3663118 ,
Doggett, Harvenna ("Bonnie") Whiteman 366311411
Doggett, Hayden James 36631141713
Doggett, Heather Jo 36631141611
Doggett, Ida Elaine 3663114113
Doggett, Isaac ("Ike") Bennett 3663111
Doggett, Jack Bryan 3663114124
Doggett, James Livy Boyd 3663114
Doggett, Janet Zulkoski 3663114114
Doggett, Jaree Nicole 3553114191
Doggett, Jed Caleb 36631141242
Doggett, Jenny Grace 3663119
Doggett, Jesse Joe 36631141131
Doggett, Jessica Jean 3663114192
Doggett, Jim Alfred 366311417
Doggett, Joanne 366311415
Doggett, John ("Dick") Morris 3663116
Doggett, John Dean 366311419
Doggett, Joy Dawn 3663114112
Doggett, Juden Rae Hamer 366311417
Doggett, Justin Luke 36631141241
Doggett, Karri Rose 36631141231
Doggett, Kathleen Elaine 3663114135
Doggett, Keegan Ray 36631143611
Doggett, Kim Milne 3663114171
Doggett, Kinzey Teneque Zarter 36631141361
Doggett, Laken Coleen 36631141262
Doggett, Linda Jo Lehman 3663114133
Doggett, Lois Jeannette Moore 3663117
Doggett, Madyson Sue 36631141921
Doggett, Maggie Marie 3663113
Doggett, Marcia Ann Edwards 3663114123
Doggett, Marjoire Irene 3663114134
Doggett, Mary Beth Summers 3663114136 .
Doggett, Mary Elizabeth 3663112
Doggett, Mary Kathryn Logian .3663114126
Doggett, Matthew Lawrence 36631141363
Doggett, Max Ray 366311411
Doggett, Michael Dean 3663114126
Doggett, Nathan Harlow 36631141711
Doggett, Oris Orlue 36631171
Doggett, Osa Mae Garretson 36631141
Doggett, Patricia 3663114162
Doggett, Patricia Cadek 366311416
Doggett, Phyllis Bartley Douglas Sime 3663114133
Doggett, Randy Robin 3663114113
Doggett, Rawley James 36631141232

Doggett, Raymond Eugene 3663114136
Doggett, Rex Lavern 3663114123
Doggett, Robert Lea 366311416
Doggett, Rodney Lee 36631141612
Doggett, Roger Dean 3663114137
Doggett, Ronald Leo 3663114161
Doggett, Rosetta Alice Podneore 3663115
Doggett, Ryan Clark 36631141244
Doggett, Sarah Jane Bennett 366311
Doggett, Shirlie Miller 366311416
Doggett, Tammy Sue Kelly 3663114137
Doggett, Teresa Ann 3663114172
Doggett, Teresa Marie Butts 3663114131
Doggett, Terrell Lavern 36631141361
Doggett, Terry Allen 3663114122
Doggett, Timothy James 36631141362
Doggett, Timothy Jay 3663114121
Doggett, Timothy Lyle 36631141234
Doggett, Tina Rae 3663114111
Doggett, Tonya Marie Walker 3663114164
Doggett, Vicki Joe Anderson 3663114124
Doggett?, Karen 3663114163
Dostal, Brian Anthony 3663114172
Dostal, Colby Paul 36631141721
Dostal, Jordan Thomas 36631141722
Dostal, Taylor Rose 36631141723
Dostal, Teresa Ann Doggett 3663114172
Driggers, Mary Ann 51331285
Driscoll, Lynn Marie 3663113243
Duenas, Ashliegh Victoria 36631172312
Duenas, Austin Zachary Moore 36631172313
Duenas, Jordan Zachary 36631172311
Duenas, Kaycee Donna Joachim 3663117231
Duenas, Zachary Vincent 3663117231
Dunlap, Jennifer Dianne Ruston 51552a232
Dunlap, Scott 51552a232
Durham, John Donald 513312812
Durham, John Michael 5133128121
Durham, Paula Kay Stewart 513312812
Durham, Tonya Ann Woods 5133128121

E

Eaves, Helen 366311231
Eddins, Amy Catherine 5133128531
Eddins, Donna Louise Walker 513312853
Eddins, Howard Burton III 513312853
Eddins, Johnathan Ross 51331285321
Eddins, Melissa Day 5133128533
Eddins, Sunny Elizabeth 5133128532
Edwards, Marcia Ann 3663114123
Elam, Martha ("Mattie") 1321x6
Eldridge, Winifred Jones 513
Emerson, George Waldo 2424452111
Emerson, Mary Stuart ("Stuey") Anderson 2424452111

F

Fanning, Candice R. Gallagher Madden 3663111211
Fanning, David 3663111211
Farmer, Annette 51331225

Farmer, Ben 51331221
Farmer, Bertha Jane Walker 5133122
Farmer, Curtis 51331222
Farmer, Mable 51331223
Farmer, Walter 513122
Farmer, William 51331224
Farrington, Ruthielee 366311735
Feldman, Jill Lynn 33631141411
Fifer, Carolyn Ann 17112221
Figueroa, Brett 36631112111
Figueroa, Garrett Nel 366311121111
Figueroa, Grant Corbett 366311121112
Figueroa, Shelley Madden 36631112111
Fleming, Susanna ("Sukey") 323
Fonville, Michael 3663114143
Fonville, Roberta Jaye Rice French Marion 3663114143
Foulger, Tracey Ann 24244522232
Freeman, Alexandra Anton Barker 323121142
Freeman, Anne Colston 32312114221
Freeman, Anne Colston Hobson 3231211422
Freeman, George Clemon, Jr. 3231211422
Freeman, George Clemon III 32312114222
Freeman, George Clemon IV 323121142223
Freeman, Joseph Reid Anderson 32312114223
Freeman, Katherine Colston 32312114222
Freeman, Louise Gilbert 32312114222
Freeman, Sara Pressly 323121142221
French, April Rae 36631141432
French, Arthur 3663114143
French, Brie Diamond 366311414311
French, Heidi Ann 36631141431
French, Roberta Jaye Rice 3663114143
Frey, Barbara Ann Jahns 366311737
Frey, Dustin Wade 366311737
Frey, Jared Michael 3663117371
Frey, Jordan Anne 3663117372
Fuller, Margie Emma Jane 5133128

G

Gallagher, Candice R. 3663111211
Gallagher, Dorothy Elaine Schuman 355311121
Gallagher, Jaree Nicole Doggett 3663114191
Gallagher, Rodney 366311121
Gallagher, Sean Justin 3663114191
Gallagher, Zaine Killien Maxwell 36631141912
Gallagher, Zoe Paityn Justine 3663114191
Garcia, Braulio 2424452655
Garcia, Tanya Georgine Mead 2424452655
Garretson, Osa Mae 36631141
Gates, Rebecca Jane Wilkinson 57363
Gates, Thomas J. 57363
Gentry, John Mark 5133128323
Gentry, Joshua Allen 51331283221
Gentry, Judith Sue Walker 513312832
Gentry, Mark 513312832
Gentry, Melissa Sue 5133128322
Gentry, Robert Walker 5133128321
Gentry, Sara Elaine Cox 5133128323

Gerhart, Virginia Buchanan 24244524152
Gilbert, Louise 32312114222
Glendening, Betty L. 366311232
Gonzolez, Mariaelena 3663113522
Gossard, Edna Rhae 1711222
Grayson, Elizabeth Cabell 132118
Grayson, Hebe Carter 132116
Grayson, Hebe Carter 13213
Grayson, Mary Eleanor 132112
Grayson, Mayme Grimes 13211a
Grayson, Robert Harrison Hanson 1321
Grayson, Roger Dixon 13211a
Grayson, Sophonisba ("Sophy") E. 132115
Grayson, Sophonisba E. Cabell 1321
Grayson, Susan Bailie 132114
Grayson, Susan Dixon 13211
Grayson, William Powhatan Bolling 13211
Greenawalt, Marie 51552a21
Greening, Christine Agnus Tyson 51331214
Greening, Paul 51331214
Griffith, Karrie Jeannette 3663117221
Griffith, Susan Kay Joachim 366311722
Griffith, Thomas Herbert 366311722
Grimes, Charles Milton 1321153
Grimes, Colonel 132116
Grimes, Hebe Carter Grayson DeMiller
    Butler 132116
Grimes, Mary ("Mollie") H. Watson 1321153
Grimes, Mayme 13211a
Griner, Virginia Charlene 513312822
Groves, Benjamin Allan 336311414112
Groves, David Scott 3663114141
Groves, Eric Scott 33631141412
Groves, Jason Scott 36631141411
Groves, Jill Lynn Feldman 36631141411
Groves, Nathan Scott 366311414111
Groves, Patricia Lynn Rice 3663114141
Cuerrant, Olive Pearl 641733
Gunnels, Brandon Marc 24244526333
Gunnels, Jennifer Clarke 24244526332
Gunnels, Laura Caroline 24244526331
Gutierrez, Angelina Alicia 36631141452
Gutierrez, Everado Lalo 3663114145
Gutierrez, Jamie Lee 36631141453
Gutierrez, Terry Jo Rice 3663114145
Gutierrez, Yolanda Maria 36631141451

H

Haddock, Joshua Burton 51331285322
Haddock, Marianne Ruth 51331285323
Haddock, Richard Riley 5133128532
Haddock, Sunny Elizabeth Eddins 5133128532
Hall, Sandra Lynn 513312823
Hamer, Juden Rae 366311417
Hansen, Carol 3663111111
Hansen, Carol Nelson 3663111112
Hansen, Harlan H. 366311111
Hansen, Marnie Shawn 36631111121
Hansen, Robert ("Bob") 3663111112
Hansen, Velma Schuman 366311111

Harlan, Charles Robert 51331284
Harlan, Doris Dean Walker 51331284
Harlan, Elizabeth Louise 513312841
Harlan, Margie Ann 513312842
Harlan, Mary Virginia 513312843
Harris, Cleland 6417321
Harrison, Edith Ogden 13213133
Harrison, Sophonisba Preston 132131x
Haselhorst, Brenda Jean Brown 36631141322
Haselhorst, Ray 36631141322
Hawley, Jimmy 3663113531
Hawley, Loretta Wareham 366311353
Hawley, Steven 366311353
Hawley, Suzanne 3663113532
Heinselman, Jacob Tad 3663117361
Heinselman, Kory Reed 366311736
Heinselman, Mary Catherine Jahns 366311736
Heinselman, Quinlee Catherine 3663117362
Henton, Maria Bennett 366312
Henton, Sam 366312
Herron, Jessica 36631132212
Hicks, Lorraine Marie VanDyk 51552a213
Hill, Beatrice Marie Labay 51552a22
Hill, Betsy Steger 5155
Hill, Beverly Renee Huber 51552a212
Hill, Billie Louise Sloan 51552a2
Hill, Billy Joe 51552a22
Hill, Christy Ann 51552a42
Hill, Courtney Lynn 51552a222
Hill, Daryl (Darrell) Barton 51552a1
Hill, DeEtta Jewell Byler 51552a1
Hill, Dempse Dekalb 515523
Hill, Diane Sawyer 51552a43
Hill, Dillon Peyton 51552a2411
Hill, Doris Wilden 51552a3
Hill, Edward Peyton 51552
Hill, Edward Peyton 51552a2
Hill, Edward Peyton, Jr. 515522
Hill, Evelyn Grace Nichols 51551a4
Hill, Glenn Howard 51552a212
Hill, Harriett Melissa 51552a8
Hill, Henrietta Louisa McGinnis 515522
Hill, Howard Hassie 51552a
Hill, Howard Wayne 51552a21
Hill, James Edward 51552a24
Hill, James Louise 51552x
Hill, James Peyton 51552a241
Hill, Jennifer Wendell 51552a241
Hill, Jessie Lee McGinnis 51552a
Hill, Jimmie Davidson 515521
Hill, John I. 51553
Hill, John Leovell 515526
Hill, Jon Wayne 51552a213
Hill, Joyce Ann 51552a23
Hill, Kathy 51552a41
Hill, Lorraine Marie VanDyk Hicks
    51552a213
Hill, Margaret Davidson 51552
Hill, Marie Greenawalt 51552a21
Hill, Marissa Nicole 51552a2122

Hill, Marvin Collier 515529
Hill, Mary Ann Leovell 51552
Hill, Minnie Neill 515521
Hill, Pamela Ruth 51552a211
Hill, Rebecca Renee 51552a2121
Hill, Sandra Kay Hudson 51552a24
Hill, Sarah F. 51554
Hill, Thomas J. 51551
Hill, Thomas Steger 515524
Hill, Tracy Marie 51552a221
Hill, Van McBride 515527
Hill, William 5155
Hill, William Columbus 515525
Hill, William Royce 51552a4
Hill, William Royce, Jr. 51552a43
Hindrelet, Katherine 64173242
Hobson, Anne Colston 3231211422
Hobson, Joseph Reid Anderson, Jr.
        323121142
Hobson, Mary Douthat Marshall 323121142
Hobson, Mary Marshall 323121142a
Hobson, Susan Lewis 3231211421
Hoge, Blanche Smith 2424452414
Hoge, Elizabeth ("Libba") Knight
        2424452513
Hoge, Elizabeth Addison ("Bessie")
        24244525
Hoge, Jennifer Ruth Karem 24244524112
Hoge, Mary Ellen Breen 2424452411
Hoge, Mary Stuart ("Honey") 24244523
Hoge, Rev. Peyton Harrison 2424452
Hoge, Peyton Harrison 2424452411
Hoge, Peyton Harrison V 24244524112
Hoge, Virginia Randolph Bolling 24244521
Hogmire, Cody Patrick 36631141354
Hogmire, Joel Kolbe 36631141355
Hogmire, John Michael 3663114135
Hogmire, Kathleen Elaine Doggett
        3663114135
Hogmire, Kelci Lynn 36631141352
Hogmire, Megan Marie 36631141351
Hogmire, Michela Brianne 36631141353
Holloway, Candice Rushnov 3663113231
Holloway, Edward 3663113231
Holstead, Deidre De La Croix 513312865
Holstead, George B. III 513312865
Holstead, George Burnham IV 5133128651
Holt, Minnie Nunley 641736
Honaker, Brenda Batson 513312824
Honaker, Charles Henry 5133128222
Honaker, Christopher Vernon 5133128242
Honaker, John Pleasant III 51331282
Honaker, John Pleasant IV 513312822
Honaker, John Pleasant V 5133128221
Honaker, Kenneth Don 513312824
Honaker, Kenneth Don II 5133128241
Honaker, Robert Lewis 513312823
Honaker, Robin Lynn 5133128231
Honaker, Sandra Lynn Hall 513312823
Honaker, Verus Elizabeth Walker 51331282

Honaker, Virginia Charlene Griner
        513312822
Honaker, William Allen 513312821
Hoover, Cathy Sue 366311419
Hopkins-Hubbard, Mindee Rae 3663117232
Huber, Beverly Renee 51552a212
Hudson, Sandra Kay 51552a24
Hurt, Audrey Beatrice 5736211

I

Ingles, Donald 3663112324
Ingles, Gretchen 36631123241
Ingles, Jennifer 36631123251
Ingles, Jill B. Bowlyow 3663112325
Ingles, Peggy A. Bowlyow 3663112324
Ingles, Randy 3663112325
Ingles, Sarah 36631123242
Ito, Kathleen Diane 3663114213

J

Jahns (son) 3663117351
Jahns (son) 3663117352
Jahns (son) 3663117353
Jahns, Barbara Ann 366311737
Jahns, Betty Jo Ann Doggett 36631173
Jahns, Cheryl Samples 366311731
Jahns, Connie 366311731
Jahns, David Lawrence 3663117341
Jahns, Donald William 36631173
Jahns, Donald William, Jr. 366311732
Jahns, Heather Jochum 366311738
Jahns, Iain C. 3663117382
Jahns, Jeremy Michael 3663117342
Jahns, Jonathon Cary 366311738
Jahns, Kimberly Ann 366311733
Jahns, Mary Catherine 366311736
Jahns, Matthew Karl 3663117331
Jahns, Michael Thomas 366311735
Jahns, Pamila Lynn Roe 366311734
Jahns, Patrick Lawrence 366311734
Jahns, Ruthielee Farrington 366311735
Jahns, Sophia C. 3663117381
Jahns, Tami Louise 3663117312
Jahns, Timothy Estel 366311731
Jahns, Timothy Estel, Jr. 3663117311
Jahns, William Karl 366311733
Joachim, Alan Moore 366311723
Joachim, Andrea Heather Read 3663117233
Joachim, Brett Alan 3663117232
Joachim, Dale Herbert 366311724
Joachim, Donald Philip 3663117233
Joachim, Donna Jeannette Doggett 3663117
Joachim, Frank Dale 36631172
Joachim, Jeanette Ruth 3663117251
Joachim, Karen Jean Cameron 366311721
Joachim, Kaycee Donna 3663117231
Joachim, Michael Cary 366311721
Joachim, Mindee Rae Hopkins-Hubbard
        3663117232
Joachim, Patricia Gail 3663117211
Joachim, Rebekah Kathleen 3663117253

Joachim, Robert Dana 366311725
Joachim, Scott Allen 366311252
Joachim, Susan Elaine Allen 366311725
Joachim, Susan Kay 366311722
Joachim, Susan Marie 3663117212
Joachim, Vickie Marlene Klingbeil
 366311723
Jochum, Heather 366311738
Johnson, _____ Thomson 5134
Johnson, Amy 36631123222
Johnson, Angela 33631123221
Johnson, Bonnie S. Bowlyow 3663112322
Johnson, Dale Edward 3663117211
Johnson, Deborah Lee 36631172112
Johnson, Holly Sue Caldwell 3663114215
Johnson, Katelin Jean 36631142152
Johnson, Loren 3663112322
Johnson, Michael David 36631172111
Johnson, Patricia Gail Joachim 3663117211
Johnson, Theodore Allen 3663114215
Johnson, Theodore Allen, Jr. 36631142151
Johnson, William E. 5134
Jones, G. M. 5133124
Jones, Lillie Elizabeth Walker 5133124

K

Karem, Jennifer Ruth 24244524112
Kauffman, Pearl Louise 17112213
Kease, Patricia Helen 21936131
Keibler, Mr. 366311319
Keibler, Phyllis Shellhammer 336311319
Kelly, Letha 5133129
Kelly, Tammy Sue 3663114137
Kerns, Margaret 171122
Kight, Chelsea 36631135231
Kight, Judy Lynn Wareham 3663113523
Kight, Kaelyn 3663223532
Kight, Kelly Kordel 3663113523
Killin, Pamela Sue 17112214
Kirkland, Ann Elizabeth 5736
Klingbeil, Vickie Marlene 366311723
Knavert, George Harrison 242445232112
Knavert, Lillian Ward 242445232113
Knight, Evelyn Tyson 51331215
Knight, Harold 51331216
Koehn, Kaden Thomas 36631172212
Koehn, Karrie Jeannette Griffith
 3663117221
Koehn, Kierra Renae 36631172211
Koehn, William C. 3663117221
Kurtzer, Cherry LaRae 36631141111
Kurtzer, Rodney Darrell 3663114111
Kurtzer, Tina Rae Doggett 3663114111
Kurtzer, Wendy Lee 36631141112
Kurtzer, Will Landon 36631141113

L

Labay, Beatrice Marie 51552a22
Lambirth, Jenny Grace Doggett 3663119
Lambirth, Lafayette 3663119

Lay, Celeste Isabella 51331283231
Lech, Brennan Ray 366311413251
Lech, Cali Marie 366311413254
Lech, Cari Marie Brown 36631141325
Lech, Daniel James 36631141325
Lech, Jacob John 366311413253
Lech, Paiton James 366311413252
Lech, Regan Danielle 336311413255
Lee, Marguerite ("Peggy") Diane 3663114211
Lehman, Linda Jo 3663114133
Lenahan, Christopher 36631123253
Lenahan, Jill B. Bowlyow Ingles 3663112325
Lenahan, John 3663112325
Lenahan, Michael 36631123252
Leovell, Mary Ann 51552
Leslie, Cleland Page Brydon 64173211
Leslie, Edith Page 641732111
Leslie, Evelyn Byrd 641732112
Leslie, Leveson Gower, Jr. 64173211
Leslie, Lindsay MacLaren 641732114
Leslie, Stephen Gower 641732113
Lester, Arminda Lucille 3663114124
Lewis, Capt. Addison 323
Lewis, Susan 3231
Lewis, Susanna ("Sukey") Fleming 323
Logian, Mary Kathryn 3663114126
Ludwig, Carolyne Jeannette Rice
 3663114142
Ludwig, Merwyn 3663114142
Lum, Julie Kay 5133128312

M

MacCorkle, Edith Page Leslie 641732111
MacCorkle, Kristen Page 6417321113
MacCorkle, Sara Lyons 6417321111
MacCorkle, Torquil, Jr. 641732111
MacCorkle, Torquil III 6417321112
MacDonald, Nancy Ann 3663111311
Mackay, George Ladeen 641734
Mackay, Mary Evelyn Brydon, M.D. 641734
Macklen, Deidre De La Croix Holstead
 513312865
Macklen, James 513312865
Macklen, Mary Kathryn 5133128652
Madden, Amy 36631112112
Madden, Candice R. Gallagher 3663111211
Madden, Gerald 3663111211
Madden, Shelley 36631112111
Madson, Cheryl Ann 3663114123
Maldonado, Armando 2424452642
Maldonado, Elizabeth ("Betsy") Ellen Mead
 2424452642
Mann, Charlsye Johnette 5133128311
Manning, Justina Lynn 3663114341
Manning, Marjorie Irene Doggett 3663114134
Manning, Michael Alexander 366311413411
Manning, William Jay 3663114134
Marion, James Austin 36631141433
Marion, Lamon 3663114143

Marion, Roberta Jaye Rice French
    3663114143
Marks, Ida Mahalia 3663111
Marquiss, Eden Nicole 1711221411
Marquiss, Logene Elizabeth 1711221412
Marquiss, Richard Anthony 171122141
Marquiss, Stephanie Sue Pendleton
    171122141
Marsden, Earl 36631122
Marsden, Frank 36631124
Marsden, Georgia L. 36631123
Marsden, Jacqueline 366311241
Marsden, Jean 366311242
Marsden, Lincoln 3663112
Marsden, Marcia 3663112212
Marsden, Mary 36631122
Marsden, Mary 366311221
Marsden, Mary Elizabeth Doggett 3663112
Marsden, Max 366311221
Marsden, Mona Dixon 36631124
Marsden, Virgie L. 36631121
Marsden, Patricia 3663112211
Marshall, Mary Catherine Wilson 3231211
Marshall, Mary Douthat 323121142
Marshall, Richard Coke 3231211
Massingill, Jordan Thomas 51552a2112
Massingill, Justin Taylor 51552a2111
Massingill, Morris Taylor 51552a211
Massingill, Pamela Ruth Hill 51552a211
Mattingly, Terie Sue 3663111311
McCloskey, Susan June Stancil Paoletti
  Monaco 3663111312
McCloskey, Thomas Francis 3663111312
McCord, Andrew King 32312114212
McCord, Anne Camm 32312114213
McCord, Colin Wallace 3231211421
McCord, Elizabeth Anne 323121142122
McCord, Emily Singer 32312114212
McCord, Mary Marshall 32312114211
McCord, Rebecca Maya 323121142121
McCord, Susan Lewis Hobson 3231211421
McCoy, Don Allen 5133128322
McCoy, Melissa Sue Gentry 5133128322
McDaniel, Deena Lynn 5133128511
McEvoy, Anne Colston 323121142212
McEvoy, Anne Colston Freeman 32312114221
McEvoy, Colin 3231211421
McEvoy, George Connor 323121142211
McEvoy, John Marshall 323121142213
McEvoy, Mark Andrew 323121142214
McGinnis, Henrietta Louisa 515522
McGinnis, Jessie Lee 51552a
McKinnon, Anna Stirling 5736211122
McKinnon, Arnold Borden, Jr. 573621112
McKinnon, Arnold Borden III 5736211121
McKinnon, Lisa Stirling Talley 573621112
Mead, Adeline 366311211
Mead, Ashley Navickis 24244526111
Mead, Barbara Hoge 2424452614
Mead, Caitlee FengYi 24244526131

Mead, Ceaghan DieuLinh 24244526132
Mead, Charles ("Chip") Jackson 2424452611
Mead, Clyde 36631121
Mead, Clyde, Jr. 366311212
Mead, Elizabeth ("Betsy") Ellen 242445264
Mead, Isabel Margot 24244526521
Mead, Kenneth 366311211
Mead, Marsda 3663112112
Mead, Mary 366311212
Mead, Mary Kay 3663112121
Mead, Mary Navickis 2424452611
Mead, Ruby Eliza 2424452631
Mead, Tanya Georgine 2424452655
Mead, Virgie L. Marsden 36631121
Mead, Wanda 3663112111
Millay, Marilyn June 366311352
Miller, Amy Sue 171122131
Miller, Betty Carol Walker 513312851
Miller, James Patrick 513312851
Miller, Paige 641732311
Miller, Shirlie 366311416
Milne, Kim 3663114171
Mobley, Copeland 51331218
Mobley, Willie Margaret Tyson 51331218
Monaco, Robert II 3663111312
Monaco, Susan June Stancil Paoletti
    3663111312
Moonan, Barbara Boorman 3663113222
Moonan, Dawn 36631132221
Moonan, Deborah 3663113222
Moonan, John Robert 366311322211
Moonan, Raymond 3663113222
Moore, Carter Randolph Brydon 64173212
Moore, Cleland Randolph 641732121
Moore, John Williamson III 64173212
Moore, Lois Jeannette 3663117
Moore, Taylor Nelson 641732122
Moreno, Melissa Sue Gentry McCoy
    5133128322
Moreno, Rogelio, Jr. 5133128322
Moreno, Stephen Anthony 51331283222
Morris, Charles 36632
Morris, Sarah Ann 36631
Murray-Thriepland, Cleland Randolph Moore
    641732121
Murray-Thriepland, Mark Patrick 641732121
Murray-Thriepland, Mary Carter 641732121
Murrie, Ellen Dame 6417353
Murrie, Ellen Dane Brydon 641735
Murrie, Hilda MacLaren 6417355
Murrie, Laura Flippen 6417352
Murrie, Robert Brydon 6417351
Murrie, William Edgar 641735
Murrie, William Edgar 6417354
Myers, Cinnamon 36631113131

N

Nash, Minnie 5133123
Navickis, Mary 2424452611
Neill, Minnie 515521

R

Rader, Clarence 171121
Rader, Elizabeth 17112111
Rader, Elizabeth Bolling Pendleton 171121
Rader, Lynn P. 1711211
Rader, Margaret Ruth 1711211
Ramstad, Darla 3663114126
Read, Andrea Heather 3663117233
Reynolds, Delma Eilene 366311418
Rice, Alice Rae Doggett 366311414
Rice, Carolyne Jeannette 3663114142
Rice, Patricia Lynn 3663114141
Rice, Robert Glen 366311414
Rice, Roberta Jaye 3663114143
Rice, Sherri Lea 3663114144
Rice, Terry Jo 3663114145

Richardson, Amber Nicole 51331281112
Richardson, Ashley Lee 51331281111
Richardson, Dick 513312811
Richardson, Dick Stewart 5133128111
Richardson, Mary Eloise Stewart 513312811
Richardson, Stephanie Tackett 5133128111
Rives, Joyce Ann Hill 51552a23
Rives, Martha ("Patsy") 573
Rives, Raymond Lee 51552a23
Rives, Susan Lea 51552a233
Robers, John Alden 171122121
Roby, Hazel Boorman Rushnov 366311323
Roby, Richard 366311323
Rodgers, Ellen Dame 64173522
Rodgers, Laura Flippen Murrie 6417352
Rodgers, Laura Humphreys 64173521
Rodgers, William Clyde 6417352
Roe, Pamila Lynn 366311734
Rogalski, Arron 366311322111
Rogalski, Beth 36631132211
Rogalski, Daniel 3663113221
Rogalski, David 33631132212
Rogalski, Elsie 366311322113
Rogalski, Gayle Boorman 3663113221
Rogalski, Jessica Herron 36631132212
Rogalski, Joshua 36631122112
Rogalski, Kenneth 36631132213
Rogalski, Mark 36631132211
Rogers, Amber 1711221211
Rogers, James Allen 171122122
Rogers, Leslie 171122121
Rogers, Miles Arthur 1711221212
Rogers, Patsy Ann Pendleton 17112212
Rogers, Terrence Walker 17112212
Rohde, Jennifer Marie 5736211211
Rohde, Kristin Jennette 5736211212
Rohde, Patricia Lynn Dean 573621121
Rohde, William C. 573621121
Rose, Sandra 366311122
Roznovak, Charles 513312842
Roznovak, Margie Ann Harlan Shaffer 513312842
Roznovak, Matthew Ryan 5133128421
Roznovak, Meghan Lindsey 5133128422

Rue, Anne Camm McCord 32312114213
Rue, Ray 32312114213
Runyan, Dolly Maggie 3663116
Rushnov, Candice 3663113231
Rushnov, Hazel Boorman 366311323
Rushnov, Jennifer 36631132312
Rushnov, Stanley 366311323
Russell, Christopher Walker 5133128731
Russell, Jeremy Ray 5133128732
Russell, Mary Elizabeth Walker 513312873
Russell, Sarah Elizabeth 5133128733
Russell, Tommy Ray 513312873
Ruston, Jeanne Renee 51552a231
Ruston, Jennifer Dianne 51552a232
Ruston, Steven Cole 51552a2311
Rutten, Cynthia L. 3663114171

S

Sadler, Brandon Lindsay 5133128712
Sadler, Erin Michele 5133128711
Sadler, Paul Lindsay 513312871
Sadler, Ronda Faye Walker 513312871
Samples, Cheryl 366311731
San Germano, Emidio 24244521
San Germano, Mary ("Mary San") Randolph 242445211
San Germano, Virginia Randolph Bolling Hoge 24244521
Sanderson (daughter) 36631141621
Sanderson (daughter) 36631141622
Sanderson, Mr. 3663114162
Sanderson, Patricia Doggett 3663114162
Sawyer, Diane 51552a43
Schmidt, Jane 513312863
Schmitt (Schmidt), Donald Benjamin Cary 24244526125
Schmitt (Schmidt), Jeremiah Nathaniel 24244526128
Schmitt (Schmidt), Johannal Elizabeth 24244526127
Schmitt (Schmidt), Joshau Paul 24244526129
Schmitt (Schmidt), Mathew Oliver 24244526126
Schmitz, Amy Johnson 36631123222
Schmitz, Michael 36631123222
Schubert, Jean Flora 366311324
Schuman, August 36631111
Schuman, Donald Fred 366311122
Schuman, Dorothy Elaine 366311121
Schuman, Edith Daggett 36631112
Schuman, Fred 36631112
Schuman, Opal Daggett 366311111
Schuman, Sandra Rose 366311122
Schuman, Velma 366311111
Scofield, Denise 3663114161
Shaffer, Margie Ann Harlan 513312842
Shaffer, Peter 513312842
Shaklee, Amy Madden 36631112112
Shaklee, Troy 36631112112
Shanke, Annie S. Norment 1321148
Shanke, Charles R. 1321148

Shellhammer, Baby 366311318
Shellhammer, Ella Marie 36631135
Shellhammer, Elsie 366311312
Shellhammer, Fay 366311314
Shellhammer, Florence 366311311
Shellhammer, Frank 366311316
Shellhammer, Hazel Mildred Smeltzer 36631131
Shellhammer, John 366311313
Shellhammer, John E. 3663113
Shellhammer, Maggie Marie Doggett Smeltzer 3363113
Shellhammer, Nora Loretta 36631136
Shellhammer, Phyllis 366311319
Shellhammer, Ralph Randall 36631131
Shellhammer, Roy 366311317
Shellhammer, Twila 336311315
Sherman, Glenda Fay Pendleton 171122214
Sherman, Mr. 171122214
Shugart, Ashleigh 51331285132
Shugart, Kristen Tipton 5133128513
Shugart, Robert Todd 5133128513
Shugart, Taylor Elizabeth 51331285131
Shutt, Dale 366311332
Shutt, Donald Eugene 366311333
Shutt, Donna 3663113311
Shutt, Dorothy 366311331
Shutt, Esther Jean Smeltzer 36631133
Shutt, Frank 36631133
Sime, Phyllis Bartley Douglas 3663114133
Simons, Elaine Alvera 366311413
Singer, Emily 32312114212
Slater, Grace Langhorne 6417324
Slaughter, Alice Elizabeth Talley 573622
Slaughter, Charles Alexander 573622
Slaughter, Martha Jefferson 57365
Sloan, Billie Louise 51552a2
Smeltzer, Esther Jean 36631133
Smeltzer, Hazel Mildred 36631131
Smeltzer, James John 3663113
Smeltzer, Maggie Marie Doggett 3663113
Smeltzer, Ruth Irene 36631132
Smeltzer, William Jennings 36631134
Smith, Hebe Carter Grayson 13213
Smith, Hebe Carter Grayson Smith 13213
Smith, Jo Ann 513312813
Smith, Lillian Mary Tyson 51331211
Smith, Morgan 51331211
Smith, William Peartree 13213
Smith, William Preston 13213
Stancil, Adam Cody 33631113133
Stancil, Aileen Johanna 36631113112
Stancil, Albert Wesley 3663111311
Stancil, Angelyna Dae 336311131331
Stancil, Chantal Post 36631113133
Stancil, Cinnamon Myers 36631113131
Stancil, Clarence Loy 366311131
Stancil, Ellen 36631113131
Stancil, Gina Susan Bertrand 3663111313
Stancil, Jesse Clayton 33631113132
Stancil, Joshua Richard 36631113131

Stancil, Justin Tyler 366311131311
Stancil, Melissa Sue 36631113111
Stancil, Nancy Ann MacDonald 3663111311
Stancil, Rebecca Ann Stancil 366311131312
Stancil, Richard Dean 3663111313
Stancil, Susan June 3663111312
Stancil, Terie Sue Mattingly 3663111311
Stancil, Willa June Witt 366311131
Starnes (?), Erika 366311322222
Starnes, Daryl 33631132222
Starnes, Deborah Moonan 36631132222
Starnes, Joel 366311322221
Stassi, Amie Claire Daigle 5133128611
Stassi, Benjamin Robert 51331286111
Stassi, Robert 5133128611
Statham, Daniel W. 24244524152
Statham, Virginia Buchanan Gerhart 24244524152
Steger, Betsy 5155
Stewart, Jo Ann Smith 513312813
Stewart, Jo Eloise Walker 51331281
Stewart, Kenneth Vardell 51331281
Stewart, Mary Eloise 513312811
Stewart, Melanie Elena 5133128131
Stewart, Paula Kay 513312812
Stewart, Robert Lance 513312813
Stewart, Velita Womble 513312813
Stokes, Sally B. 219361
Stone, Jean Marsden 366311242
Stone, Richard 366311242
Street, Amanda Nicole 366311131111
Street, John Northscott III 36631113111
Street, Melissa Sue Stancil 36631113111
Sullivan, Doris Elizabeth Witt 3663111321
Sullivan, Michael John 3663111321
Summers, Ava Irene 1711221
Summers, Mary Beth 3663114136
Swallen, Evelyn Byrd Leslie 641732112
Swallen, Jeffrey Warner 641732112
Swallen, Peter Leslie 6417321121
Swallen, Richard MacLaren 6417321122
Synnott, Coral 219361311

T

Tackett, Stephanie 5133128111
Talley, Alice Elizabeth 573622
Talley, Andrew Atkins 5736211113
Talley, Audrey Beatrice Hurt 5736211
Talley, Audrey Hurt 57362112
Talley, Betty Fay White 57362111
Talley, Chastine Herod 57362
Talley, Elizabeth Baskervill 5736211112
Talley, Kathryn Paul 573621114
Talley, Lisa Stirling 573621112
Talley, Margaret Elizabeth Baskervill 573621111
Talley, Margaret Slaughter Atkins 573621
Talley, Martha Atkins 5736212
Talley, Martha Frances Wilkinson 57362
Talley, Melvin White 573621113
Talley, Virginia May 5736213